Grammar: Grades 5–6

D1371174

Table of Contents

Nouns and Pronouns
Common Nouns....................................4
Proper Nouns 5
Concrete and Abstract Nouns........6
Singular and Plural Nouns 7
Plural Nouns..8
Possessive Nouns.............................10
Subject and Object Pronouns......11
Possessive Pronouns.......................12
Reflexive Pronouns 13
Indefinite Pronouns 14
Interrogative and
    Demonstrative Pronouns 15

Verbs
Action Verbs 16
Linking Verbs.....................................17
Helping Verbs and
    Verb Phrases 18
Present, Past, and
    Future Tense Action Verbs 19
Past Tense Verbs.............................. 22
Review Present, Past, and
    Future Tense Verbs 23
Infinitives 24
Present and Past Participles......... 25
Past Participle of
    Irregular Verbs..............................26
Present Perfect, Past Perfect, and
    Future Perfect Verbs 28
Present Perfect Tense 29
Verb Tense Review 30
Present Progressive and
    Past Progressive Tenses 31

Adjectives
Adjectives...32
Demonstrative Adjectives 33

Limiting and
    Descriptive Adjectives................ 34
Comparative and
    Superlative Adjectives.................35
Predicate Adjectives 37
Articles.. 38
Appositives 40

Adverbs
Adverbs...41
Time Adverbs 42
Place Adverbs 43
Manner Adverbs............................... 44
Comparative and
    Superlative Adverbs.....................45

Punctuation
Capitalization 47
Commas 50
Hyphens and Dashes.......................52
Quotation Marks 53
Single Quotation Marks.................. 54
Apostrophes 55
Semicolons 56
Colons 57

Sentences
Parts of a Sentence......................... 58
Simple Subjects................................59
Simple Predicates 60
Simple Subjects and Predicates....61
Complete Subjects
    and Predicates...............................62
Compound Subjects........................63
Compound Predicates 64
Compound Subjects
    and Predicates...............................65
Subject-Verb Agreement 66
Prepositions......................................69

Prepositional Phrases......................70
Direct Objects 73
Indirect Objects...............................75
Clauses 77
Relative Clauses 78
Independent and
    Dependent Clauses......................79
Sentence Building with Clauses....80
Conjunctions 81
Coordinating Conjunctions..........82
Correlative Conjunctions 83
Subordinating Conjunctions 84
Building Sentences 85
Expanding Sentences.....................86
Types of Sentences.........................87
Run-On Sentences 89
Sentence Fragments...................... 90
Active and Passive Voice 91

Word Study
Double Negatives 92
Doesn't and *Don't* 93
Who and *Whom* 94
Lie/Lay and *May/Can*...................95
That and *Which* 96
Synonyms and Antonyms...............97
Homophones and Homographs... 98
Synonyms, Antonyms, Homophones,
    and Homographs.......................... 99
Idioms 100

Writing
Business Letters........................... 101
Writing Dialogue........................... 103

Answer Key................................... 104

ISBN 978-1-60418-261-3
04-301131151

Ready-to-Use Ideas and Activities

The activities in this book have been developed to help students master the basic skills necessary to succeed in grammar. These skills include learning about basic parts of speech, sentence components, and other word-study skills such as homophones and homographs. The activities have been sequenced to help ensure successful completion of the assigned tasks, thus building positive self-esteem, as well as the self-confidence students need to meet academic challenges. The activities may be used by themselves, as supplemental activities, or as enrichment material for a grammar program.

As you read through the activities listed below and go through this book, remember that all children learn at their own rate. Although repetition is important, it is critical that we keep sight of the fact that it is equally important to build children's self-esteem and self-confidence to become successful learners. If you are working with a child at home, set up a quiet, comfortable environment where you will work. Make it a special time to which you each look forward. Do only a few activities at a time and end each session on a positive note.

Flash Card Ideas
Cut apart the flash cards provided in the back of this book and use them for basic skill and enrichment activities. You can use them in the following ways or create your own way to use them.

- Write some or all of the flash card words where they can be seen and divide students into groups. As students look at the list of words, describe a word from the list. Begin with the part of speech, and then use synonyms, antonyms, spelling characteristics, a definition, how the word makes you feel, what kind of emotion it evokes, or anything else you can think of that describes the word. The team who correctly guesses the word first wins one point. After each word is guessed correctly, cross it off the list and go on to another. You can either have the group try to guess the word together or rotate guessers, giving everyone a chance. Continue playing to a certain number or until only one word remains.

 CD-104311 • © Carson-Dellosa

Ready-to-Use Ideas and Activities

- Create a bingo sheet with five rows and five columns of blank squares. Write *FREE* in the middle square. Make enough copies to give one to each student. Write the flash card words as a list where students can see them. Have students choose 24 words from the list and write the words in the empty spaces of their bingo cards.

  When students have finished filling out their bingo cards, make the flash cards into a deck. Call out the words one at a time. If a student has the word on his card, he should mark an *X* through the word to cross it out. The student who first crosses out five words in a row—horizontally, vertically, or diagonally—wins the game when she shouts, "Bingo!"

  To extend the game, continue playing until a student crosses out all of the words on his bingo sheet.

- Give each student three or four cards. Call out a part of speech (noun, verb, adjective, etc.) and have students hold up words that belong to that category.

- Have students categorize the words into designated groups. Use the categorized groups to create sentences.

- Have students alphabetize the cards as they read the words aloud.

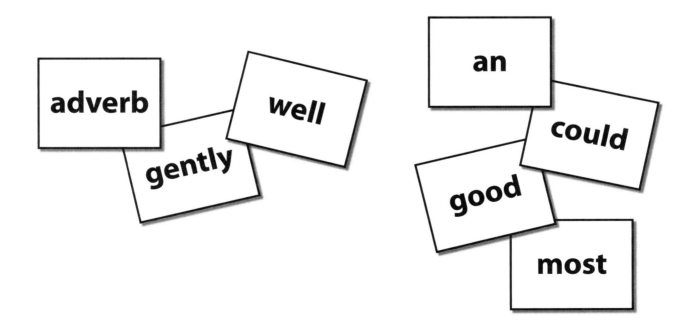

Common Nouns

A **common noun** is a word that names a person, place, or thing.
Examples: girl (person), kitchen (place), window (thing)

Write each common noun under the correct heading.

teacher	pharmacy	lawyer
cabinet	studio	thermometer
cone	lobby	soldier
park	daisy	partner
university	satellite	salesperson
picture	infant	mainland

People	**Places**	**Things**
_____	_____	_____
_____	_____	_____
_____	_____	_____
_____	_____	_____
_____	_____	_____
_____	_____	_____

Proper Nouns

> A **proper noun** is a word that names a specific person, place, or thing. The first letter of a proper noun is capitalized.
>
> Examples: Susan (specific person), Canada (specific place), *Little House on the Prairie* (specific thing)

Circle the common nouns and underline the proper nouns in each sentence.

1. The roof on the old barn is peeling.

2. A row of ants marched across the picnic blanket.

3. My mom loves to visit Myrtle Beach in South Carolina.

4. Walter put on his boots before going outside.

5. Do alligators live in swamps?

6. Jack wants to visit Paris, France.

7. Samantha checked out three books from the library.

8. Tom likes to eat at a restaurant called Good Eating.

9. Is Juan going to the store with Jamil?

10. The dance will take place in the school gym.

11. The computer in the library works best.

12. My cousin Jackie lives in Toronto, Canada.

Concrete and Abstract Nouns

> A **concrete noun** identifies something that can be seen, heard, smelled, touched, or tasted.
>
>   Examples: popcorn, theater, music
>
> An **abstract noun** is a word that names an idea or quality that cannot be physically interacted with.
>
>   Examples: memory, kindness, love

Write C for each concrete noun and A for each abstract noun.

1. joy   _____

2. bravery   _____

3. hair   _____

4. imagination _____

5. peach   _____

6. freedom   _____

7. shout   _____

8. guitar   _____

Decide if the noun *pride* is a concrete noun or an abstract noun. Explain your decision.

_____

_____

Singular and Plural Nouns

A **singular noun** names one person, place, thing, or idea.

A **plural noun** names more than one person, place, thing, or idea.

Add *s* to most singular nouns to make them plural.

    Example: book → books

If a singular noun ends with *sh, ch, x, s,* or *z,* add *es* to make it plural.

    Example: beach → beaches

If a singular noun ends with a consonant followed by *y,* change the *y* to *i* and add *es* to make the word plural.

    Example: baby → babies

If the singular noun ends with a vowel followed by *y,* just add *s* to make the plural.

    Example: boy → boys

Write the plural form of each singular noun.

1. crash _____

2. comic _____

3. lady _____

4. dentist _____

5. suggestion _____

6. decision _____

7. address _____

8. branch _____

9. glimpse _____

10. responsibility _____

11. business _____

12. tax _____

13. poster _____

14. dress _____

15. tortilla _____

16. melody _____

Name _____

Plural Nouns

Complete each sentence with the plural form of the noun in parentheses.

1. Many people are interested in ancient _____. (mystery)

2. One mystery concerns gigantic stone _____ on Easter Island. (statue)

3. The stone _____ were all carved inside an extinct volcano. (figure)

4. Scientists wonder how the _____ of the island could have moved the 30-ton pieces from the volcano to other positions on the island. (resident)

5. They all look alike, with deep eye sockets but no _____. (eye)

6. Their _____ are long, and their chins are pointed. (earlobe)

7. They are thought to have been _____ to remember certain people. (monument)

8. The statues attract visitors from many _____. (country)

9. _____ reach the island by airplane or sailboat. (traveler)

10. There are _____ to sleep and eat on the island too. (place)

Name _____

Plural Nouns

Write the plural form of each singular noun.

1. stereo _____

2. juice _____

3. watch _____

4. wife _____

5. wolf _____

6. shelf _____

7. puppy _____

8. baby _____

9. hobby _____

10. glass _____

11. boy _____

12. bay _____

13. domino _____

14. hero _____

15. sandwich _____

16. wash _____

17. fox _____

18. calf _____

19. radio _____

20. cry _____

21. city _____

22. jelly _____

23. strawberry _____

24. chimney _____

25. toy _____

26. turkey _____

27. potato _____

28. video _____

Possessive Nouns

A **possessive noun** shows ownership or belonging.

If a noun is singular or if it is plural but does not end with an *s*, add an apostrophe plus an *s* (*'s*) to the end to make it possessive.

    Examples: dog's food, teacher's pen, men's belts

If a noun is plural and ends with an *s*, add an apostrophe (') to the end.

    Examples: cats' collars, dancers' shoes

Change each phrase into a phrase that uses a possessive noun.

Example: the car belonging to the family ⟶ the family's car

1. the toys belonging to the brothers

_____

2. the brush belonging to Iris

_____

3. the doll belonging to the twins

_____

4. the bike belonging to his sister

_____

Circle each possessive noun. Write *S* if it is singular possessive or *P* if it is plural possessive.

_____ 5. The dog's new leather collar is lost.

_____ 6. The snails' aquarium needed cleaning.

_____ 7. The art project's colors were faded by the sun.

_____ 8. The copier is in the teachers' workroom.

Subject and Object Pronouns

A **subject pronoun** is a pronoun that replaces a noun as the subject of a sentence.

He, she, it, we, and *they* are examples of subject pronouns that can replace nouns or phrases with nouns in the subject of a sentence.

  Example: *Robert Browning* was a poet. → *He* was a poet.

You and *I* are examples of subject pronouns that do not need a reference to the noun or phrase that they are replacing.

  Example: *You* and *I* enjoy his poetry.

An **object pronoun** is a pronoun that replaces a noun in the predicate of a sentence.

Him, her, it, us, and *them* are examples of object pronouns that can replace a noun or phrase with nouns in the predicate of a sentence.

  Example: Robert Browning married *Elizabeth Barrett* in 1846. →
  Robert Browning married *her* in 1846.

You and *me* are examples of object pronouns that do not need a reference to the noun or phrase that they are replacing.

  Example: Mother reads the Brownings' poetry to *you* and *me*.

Rewrite each sentence using a subject or object pronoun for each underlined word or phrase.

1. Robert was interested in writing about <u>people who lived in the past</u>.

  _____

2. <u>Elizabeth Barrett Browning</u> was a poet during the Victorian period in England.

  _____

3. <u>Robert</u> admired her poetry, and he wrote to Elizabeth.

  _____

4. <u>Robert and Elizabeth</u> were married in 1846.

  _____

Possessive Pronouns

> A **possessive pronoun** is a pronoun that takes the place of a possessive noun. A possessive pronoun does not have an apostrophe.
>
> Example: *Erin's* brush is on the table. → *Her* brush is on the table.
>
> Possessive pronouns: my, your, his, her, its, our, their, mine, yours, his, hers, ours, theirs

Circle each possessive pronoun. Draw an arrow to the noun that it modifies.

1. Their mom travels around the state on business.

2. Our house is near the library.

3. Its handle is loose.

4. The black dog beside the tree is mine.

5. Her socks are in the middle drawer.

6. We went to the musical with his parents.

7. The house with the pool is his.

8. My friend asked my opinion about which bike to buy.

9. The salami and cheese sandwich is hers.

10. Their wooded backyard is a great place to play.

11. Her older cousin is staying at a hotel for a week.

12. The trophy has its own shelf.

Name _____

Reflexive Pronouns

A **reflexive pronoun** is a pronoun that reflects the action of the verb back to the subject.

Singular reflexive pronouns: myself, yourself, itself, herself, himself
> Example: Leonardo da Vinci painted with a style that made the painting *itself* look misty.

Plural reflexive pronouns: ourselves, yourselves, themselves
> Example: You all can see the painting's soft and muted colors for *yourselves*.

Write the reflexive pronoun in each sentence on the line.

1. The woman in Leonardo da Vinci's painting, the *Mona Lisa*, seems to be smiling to herself.

_____

2. For centuries, people have asked themselves why this is so. _____

3. I have wondered myself about her mysterious smile. _____

4. Leonardo da Vinci kept that secret to himself. _____

5. If you want to see the *Mona Lisa* for yourself, go to the Louvre Museum in Paris, France.

_____

Complete each sentence with the correct pronoun in parentheses.

6. Leonardo developed a new painting technique all by _____. (itself, himself)

7. The wall _____ was Leonardo's canvas. (himself, itself)

8. I have tried the technique _____ and found it challenging. (myself, ourselves)

Indefinite Pronouns

> An **indefinite pronoun** is a pronoun that refers to a noun in a general way.
> Examples: all, another, any, anybody, anyone, anything, both, each, either, everybody, everyone, everything, few, little, many, much, neither, nobody, none, no one, nothing, one, other, others, several, some, somebody, someone, something

Circle the indefinite pronouns in each sentence.

1. Many will come to the museum this summer.

2. A hummingbird came to the feeder this morning, and another came last night.

3. Someone got the crowd cheering excitedly.

4. Only a few registered, but several arrived on the day of the race.

5. I think somebody should clean up the marbles and game pieces.

6. Walter and Mason are here with a mower; either can mow the yard.

7. If anybody gets home before me, they can put dinner in the oven.

8. Fruits and vegetables are delicious; each is good for a healthy, growing body.

9. Jessie really wanted to eat both types of cheese.

10. Some have blue tags, and others have red tags.

11. Nothing can be done about the misplaced invitation.

12. All leaves will fall from the trees at the end of summer.

13. Anyone can go to the amusement park.

14. Several swam downstream into the lake.

Interrogative and Demonstrative Pronouns

An **interrogative pronoun** is a pronoun that introduces a question.

Interrogative pronouns: who, whom, whose, which, what
> Examples: *Who* is he? *Whom* do you see? *Whose* is this?
> *Which* of you can help me? *What* is the answer?

A **demonstrative pronoun** identifies and specifies a noun or pronoun.

Demonstrative pronouns: this, that, these, and those
> Examples: *This* is nice. *That* is nicer. *These* are fine. *Those* are finer.

Complete each sentence with the correct pronoun in parentheses.

1. _____ is a fact. (This, These)

2. _____ are little pictures. (That, Those)

3. _____ is the importance of grammar? (What, Which)

4. _____ are not my shoes. (This, These)

5. _____ is an interesting idea. (Those, That)

6. _____ were some of the things you did on vacation? (Whom, What)

7. _____ do you know? (That, Whom)

8. _____ were some of the earliest paintings found in Mexico? (Who, What)

9. _____ are your pancakes. (Those, Whose)

10. _____ celebration do you like best? (Which, That)

Action Verbs

> An **action verb** is a word that expresses action.
> Examples: The audience *applauds* enthusiastically.
> Maria *runs* fast.

Underline the action verb in each sentence.

1. Julie camps in the mountains every summer.

2. Celia finishes her math assignment.

3. She scours the newspaper for the best sales.

4. Mario reviews his answers for each test question.

5. The cow quietly chews the grass.

6. Cynthia picks tomatoes from her garden all summer.

7. Please change the flat tire for me.

8. The sign dangles in the window.

9. The baby squeals with happiness.

10. Mr. Andrews spots the monkey in the tree.

11. Are you watching the football game tonight?

12. My cat drinks water from the faucet outside.

13. Kayla hangs the laundry outside to dry.

14. Lincoln rides his bike for exercise.

Linking Verbs

> A **linking verb** is a verb that does not show action. It links or joins the subject of a sentence to information about the subject.
>
> Forms of the verb *be* are the most common linking verbs. There are eight forms of the verb *be:* am, are, is, was, were, (will) be, (am, are, was, were) being, (have, has, had) been.
>
>   Example: The soup *is* wonderful.
>
> Other linking verbs include forms of these verbs: appear, become, feel, grow, look, remain, seem, smell, sound, taste.
>
>   Example: The soup *tastes* wonderful.

Underline the linking verb in each sentence.

1. The knitted mittens are very warm.

2. The food on the table appears fresh.

3. The neighbor's dog was sprayed by a skunk.

4. The garbage can by the door is full.

5. That frozen dessert tastes fruity.

6. The letters my mother sent grow more special to me every year.

7. Haley, April's big sister, is our junior counselor.

8. Amber, my younger cousin, will be in first grade next year.

9. The moon was like a huge orange ball hovering in the sky.

10. The music grew increasingly louder.

11. Ms. Tolio, my mom's friend, is a pediatric surgeon.

12. Mom's new scissors are sharp enough to cut cardboard.

13. Dr. Grogan, my orthodontist, is nice.

14. Last night, the moon was low in the sky.

Helping Verbs and Verb Phrases

Helping verbs are verbs that help main verbs tell when the action takes place.

There are 23 helping verbs:

be, am, are, is, was, were, being, been	may, must, might
do, does, did	will, can, shall
have, has, had	could, would, should

Up to three helping verbs can precede the main verb. The main verb together with its helping verb or verbs makes a verb phrase.

Example: I *will talk* to my friend.

I *will have talked* to my friend.

I *will have been talking* to my friend.

Circle the helping verbs in each sentence. Underline the verb phrases.

1. Sari did jump on the trampoline.

2. The water is pouring into the basement.

3. The rabbit had scurried into the hole.

4. We are going to the amusement park.

5. I am excited to be here.

6. The lights can be dimmed with this switch.

7. Max was taking his turn.

8. The puppy must have tried to jump onto the bed.

9. That jam would make a good sandwich.

10. The bird had flown into the bushes.

11. We should pull the weeds out of the garden.

12. Emma may have been going to the zoo.

Name _____

Present, Past, and Future Tense Action Verbs

Verb tenses tell when the action of a verb happens.

A **present tense action verb** tells about an action that is happening now.
  Example: Companies *develop* new medicines from plants.

A **past tense action verb** tells about an action that has already happened.
  Example: People *discovered* that many plants could cure illnesses.

A **future tense action verb** tells about an action that will happen in the future.
  Example: People *will continue* to search for new medicines.

Circle the action verb in each sentence. Write the tense (present, past, or future) of the action verb on the line.

1. The barber cuts Owen's hair. _____

2. I will study hard for the test tomorrow. _____

3. Tim carried his own luggage to the security gate. _____

4. Barney suddenly leaped into the air for no good reason. _____

5. She talks with her mom about dinner. _____

6. Natasha will turn 12 next week. _____

7. Aaron planted tomatoes, peppers, and cucumbers in his garden. _____

8. Melody will laugh when she reads my birthday card. _____

9. Ms. McGuire listens to the radio in the morning. _____

Present, Past, and Future Tense Action Verbs

Write *past, present,* or *future* to identify the tense of the underlined action verb.

1. Queen Elizabeth I <u>reigned</u> during England's Golden Age. _____

2. Ms. Wong <u>handed</u> the supplies for the experiment to the students. _____

3. The seamstress <u>measures</u> the fabric for her son's suit. _____

4. He <u>submerged</u> his sprained ankle in a bucket of ice water. _____

5. I <u>will fill</u> your glass with milk. _____

6. Many cosmetics <u>contain</u> plant ingredients. _____

7. The light <u>streams</u> through my windows. _____

8. A pacemaker <u>regulates</u> a person's heartbeat. _____

9. One key on my calculator <u>stayed</u> down when I released it. _____

10. This Web site <u>will help</u> you research historical figures. _____

Present, Past, and Future Tense Action Verbs

Underline the action verb in each sentence. If the action verb is future tense, underline both the action verb and the helping verb *will*. Circle *past, present,* or *future* for each action verb.

1. The barrel collects rainwater.	past	present	future
2. Jamie writes to her friend.	past	present	future
3. Layne will make the popcorn.	past	present	future
4. Jackie planted vegetables in the garden.	past	present	future
5. Marco will arrange the flowers.	past	present	future
6. The soup boiled over onto the stove.	past	present	future
7. Chris will lounge in the hammock.	past	present	future
8. The machine chopped the tree limb.	past	present	future
9. The driver pulled into the parking space.	past	present	future
10. Hailey placed the card on the table.	past	present	future
11. The chef prepares dinner.	past	present	future
12. A jellyfish floats on the waves.	past	present	future

Past Tense Verbs

Remember, the past tense is used to show action that has already happened.

Usually, *ed* or *d* is added to a verb to form the past tense.

Examples: walk → walked

wave → waved

If a verb ends with a consonant + *y,* change *y* to *i* and add *ed.*

Example: carry → carried

If a verb has a short vowel with one consonant, double the consonant and add *ed.*

Examples: hop → hopped

stop → stopped

Write the past tense of each verb.

1. rustle _____

2. bat _____

3. lunge _____

4. agree _____

5. ship _____

6. end _____

7. cry _____

8. sip _____

9. snap _____

10. create _____

Complete each sentence with the past tense of the verb in parentheses.

11. Julio _____ his work onto clean paper. (copy)

12. The kitten _____ on the ladybug. (pounce)

13. Quincy _____ spinach for the first time. (try)

14. Paulo _____ to his piano lesson. (hurry)

15. Annabelle _____ a game with her cousin. (play)

16. Brett _____ for comfortable shoes. (shop)

Review Present, Past, and Future Tense Verbs

Complete the chart.

Present	Past	Future
1. climb	_____	_____
2. vary	_____	_____
3. _____	planned	_____
4. _____	_____	will browse
5. _____	argued	_____
6. lecture	_____	_____
7. _____	delayed	_____
8. _____	_____	will promote
9. arrange	_____	_____
10. _____	owned	_____
11. _____	_____	will travel
12. ponder	_____	_____

Infinitives

A verb has four principal parts: present (infinitive), present participle, past, and past participle.

An **infinitive** is the *to* form of a verb. It is composed of the word *to* and what is called the base form, or most basic form, of a verb.

Examples: to be

to sleep

to eat

Circle the infinitives in each sentence.

1. We need to water the plants.

2. Lee's goal was to be outstanding.

3. It takes strength to open the jar.

4. You will need to remove the plastic liner.

5. A ticket is needed to enter the movie theater.

6. My friend brought a game for us to play.

7. We want to enjoy the movie without a lot of extra noise.

8. Many people like to drink from the drinking fountain.

9. Abby and Pearl want to show the class how to make pancakes.

10. We will be ready to leave when all of the toys are picked up.

11. The buds on the yellow flowers are beginning to open.

12. Dad is driving across town to buy more wood.

Present and Past Participles

The **present participle** is formed by adding *ing* to the base form of a verb.

   Example: Base form: rock —► Present participle: rocking

The **past participle** is usually formed by adding *ed* or *d* to the base form of a verb and is the same as the past tense form of the verb.

   Example: Base form: rock —► Past participle: rocked

Some irregular verbs have past participles that are not formed by adding *ed* or *d* and may not be the same as the past tense form of the verb.

   Example: Base form: see —► Past participle: seen

Complete the chart.

Present	Present Participle	Past	Past Participle
1. work	_____	_____	_____
2. walk	_____	_____	_____
3. view	_____	_____	_____
4. call	_____	_____	_____
5. plant	_____	_____	_____
6. leap	_____	_____	_____

Draw a line to the correct past participle of each irregular verb.

7. break	chosen
8. tear	broken
9. bring	gone
10. choose	begun
11. go	brought
12. begin	torn

Past Participle of Irregular Verbs

The past participle of an irregular verb can be the same as or different from the past tense form of the verb. Past participles of irregular verbs often end with *t, en,* or *n.*

Examples:	Present	Past	Past Participle
	ring	rang	rung
	wear	wore	worn
	blow	blew	blown

Complete each sentence with the correct past participle in the parentheses.

1. The mother blue jay has _____ on her eggs for many days. (sitted, sat)

2. Mr. Wu has _____ to take the subway to work this morning. (chose, chosen)

3. The towering old pine had _____ during the snowstorm. (fell, fallen)

4. Rick has _____ on the phone for two hours. (spoked, spoken)

5. The girls had _____ on the tire swing before us. (swinged, swung)

6. Ralph and Perry have _____ in Lake Michigan before. (swimmed, swum)

7. The goat at the zoo had _____ the food on the ground. (ate, eaten)

8. Tyrone had _____ his camera on the picnic table. (setted, set)

9. The mother of the groom has _____ the wedding cake. (maked, made)

10. The fishermen had _____ before the sun came up. (arosed, risen)

11. Cyndi has _____ several butterflies in her net. (catched, caught)

12. That hornet had _____ Sasha's hand. (stinged, stung)

13. Xena and Sean _____ down the snowy hill on their sled. (slided, slid)

14. The vase has _____ into pieces on the floor. (broke, broken)

Past Participle of Irregular Verbs

Fill in the chart with the correct forms of the irregular verbs. Refer to a dictionary, if needed.

Present	Past	Past Participle
1. draw	_____	_____
2. _____	swam	_____
3. _____	_____	taught

Complete each sentence with the past tense of the irregular verb in parentheses.

4. Two men _____ at the foot of the Pennine Alps. (stand)

5. Heavy snow _____, and the storm raged around them. (fall)

6. They _____ only snow, ice, and the mountain. (see)

Complete each sentence with the past participle of the irregular verb in parentheses.

7. They have _____ of climbing the mountain for months. (think)

8. The men have _____ it would be difficult to climb at this time of year. (know)

9. They have _____ to wait to climb until the weather is clear. (choose)

Present Perfect, Past Perfect, and Future Perfect Verbs

The **present perfect tense** of a verb indicates action that has been completed or that extends into the present. It is formed by adding the word *have* or *has* before the past participle.

Examples: I *have gone* to that shop before.

Julio *has gone* to that shop before.

The **past perfect tense** of a verb indicates action that was completed before something else happened. It is formed by adding the word *had* before the past participle.

Examples: I *had gone* by the time he arrived.

Julio *had gone* by the time he arrived.

The **future perfect tense** of a verb indicates action that will have been completed in the future before something else happens. It is formed by adding the words *will have* before the past participle.

Examples: I *will have gone* by the time he arrives.

Julio *will have gone* by the time he arrives.

Rewrite each sentence using the perfect tense for each verb in parentheses.

1. Since Tommy _____ his homework, he was free the rest of the evening. (do, past perfect)

   _____

   _____

2. I _____ a marathon two months before I run the Boston Marathon. (run, future perfect)

   _____

   _____

3. Mom _____ countless numbers of doors for me since I broke my leg. (open, present perfect)

   _____

   _____

4. Reenie said they _____ to Connecticut five times after they take their trip. (go, future perfect)

   _____

   _____

Present Perfect Tense

Write the present perfect tense of the verb in parentheses in each sentence.

1. Lightning _____ a fire in Yellowstone National Park. (start)

2. The old spruce and fir trees _____ quickly. (burn)

3. Flaming twigs _____ dry leaves on the forest floor. (ignite)

4. The winds _____ up, and the fire has intensified. (pick)

5. The wildfire _____ up the valley rapidly. (move)

6. The governor _____ that many counties evacuate. (request)

7. Organizations _____ people to gather items for families in need. (urge)

8. The teachers, staff, and students at my school _____ many items to help people. (donate)

9. Many people _____ the families during this difficult time. (help)

10. I hope that the firefighters _____ the fire. (extinguish)

Verb Tense Review

Circle the verb in each sentence below. Then, identify the tense of each verb. Use the abbreviations below.

SPRE—simple present	SF—simple future
PASTP—past perfect	SPAST—simple past
PREP—present perfect	FP—future perfect

_____ 1. Kenzie had seen the other team arrive before the game.

_____ 2. I will support Andrew for our student government representative.

_____ 3. The wind blows rapidly this time of year.

_____ 4. Can I please study with you next time?

_____ 5. Marie will have gone home by then!

_____ 6. Alexander Graham Bell invented the telephone in 1876.

_____ 7. Lexie had talked to Mr. Brown about her math test after school.

_____ 8. The team had hoped for more wins this year.

_____ 9. The students have studied for many hours for the test.

_____ 10. Renee has talked with the guidance counselor.

_____ 11. Mom will follow us to the restaurant.

_____ 12. David has decided to buy the yellow hat.

Present Progressive and Past Progressive Tenses

The **present progressive tense** of a verb tells about ongoing action happening in the present.

Use forms of *be* (*am, is,* and *are*) with the present participle to form the present progressive tense.

   Example: The clouds *are growing* in intensity.

The **past progressive tense** of a verb tells about an ongoing action that happened in the past and is now completed.

Use past tense forms of *be* (*was* and *were*) with the present participle to form the past progressive tense.

   Example: The winds *were beginning* to change direction.

Write each sentence twice. Write the first with the present progressive tense of the verb in parentheses. Write the second with the past progressive tense of the verb in parentheses.

The scientist _____ the discovery of fossils in the ground. (explain)

1. _____

2. _____

The ballerinas _____ into the air. (leap)

3. _____

4. _____

Dan _____ for our teacher today. (substitute)

5. _____

6. _____

Adjectives

An **adjective** is a word that describes a noun. It answers *How many? What kind?* or *Which one?*

An adjective often comes in front of the noun it describes.
　　Example: The *red* kayak bobbed up and down.

An adjective can come after a linking verb. A linking verb connects the subject part of a sentence with an adjective in the predicate.
　　Example: The river was *white* with foam.

A sentence may have more than one adjective.
　　Example: *Foaming, swirling* waters were ahead of us.

Circle the adjective or adjectives that describe the underlined noun or nouns.

1. White-water kayaking is a thrilling <u>adventure</u>.

2. A kayak is a boat with a closed <u>top</u>.

3. The small boat is guided by a person using a two-bladed <u>paddle</u>.

4. Wearing a protective <u>helmet</u> is mandatory.

5. It is a good idea for paddlers to wear an inflatable <u>vest</u> too.

6. A wet suit is important to wear in icy mountain <u>streams</u>.

7. What is it like to challenge a raging <u>river or stream</u>?

8. It takes strength and skill to guide a kayak through jagged <u>rocks</u>.

9. There may be swift, treacherous <u>currents</u>.

10. Kayak with experienced <u>paddlers</u>—never alone.

Demonstrative Adjectives

A **demonstrative adjective** answers *Which one? This, that, these,* and *those* are examples of demonstrative adjectives.

Circle the demonstrative adjective in each sentence. Draw an arrow from each demonstrative adjective to the noun it describes.

Example: These peanuts are salted.

1. Those scented candles produce very hot wax.

2. That four-year-old child chatters constantly.

3. This fuzzy peach has a bruised spot.

4. Those majestic glaciers tower above the cruise ship.

5. That dirty blue sock has a small hole in the toe.

6. This yellow pencil has a broken point.

7. My little sister is in that class.

8. Barney wants that chocolate cupcake with white frosting.

9. Vera drew that sketch of the storm clouds.

10. These tiny black seeds can grow delicious white radishes.

11. Those glass marbles belong to the boy.

12. That black camera takes great photographs.

Limiting and Descriptive Adjectives

A **descriptive adjective** adds details to a noun and answers *What kind?*

Examples: *shabby* couch, *honest* friend

A **limiting adjective** tells a quantity or number and answers *How many?*

Examples: *one* sign, a *few* apples

Underline each descriptive adjective and circle each limiting adjective.

1. Our dog had four puppies.

2. I love to sit in front of a crackling fire.

3. Let's toast delicious marshmallows!

4. I need five notebooks for school.

5. Did you see the spotted leopard?

6. May I have two more cookies?

7. I would like a glass of cold milk.

8. Please hand me a few grapes.

Comparative and Superlative Adjectives

Some adjectives compare nouns.

A **comparative adjective** compares two nouns. Usually, a comparative adjective is formed by adding *er* to an adjective.

Example: tall —▶ taller

A **superlative adjective** compares more than two nouns. Usually, a superlative adjective is formed by adding *est* to an adjective.

Example: short —▶ shortest

If an adjective ends with *e,* drop the *e* and add *er* or *est.*

Example: rare —▶ rarest

If an adjective ends in a consonant + *y,* change *y* to *i* and add *er* or *est.*

Example: funny —▶ funnier

If an adjective has a short vowel and ends with one consonant, double the consonant and add *er* or *est.*

Example: mad —▶ madder

If an adjective has two or more syllables, use *more, most, less,* or *least* before it.

Example: wonderful —▶ most wonderful

Write the comparative and superlative forms of each adjective.

	Comparative	Superlative
1. happy	_____	_____
2. wise	_____	_____
3. fast	_____	_____
4. great	_____	_____
5. delicious	_____	_____
6. interesting	_____	_____
7. vibrant	_____	_____
8. majestic	_____	_____

Comparative and Superlative Adjectives

Circle the correct form of the adjective in each sentence.

1. The (nearest, more near) restaurant is four miles away.

2. This hot chocolate is (hotter, most hot) than I like it.

3. My friend Pedro is the (most nice, nicest) person I know.

4. That movie was (funnier, funniest) than the one we watched last week.

5. This book is (intense, less intense) than its sequel.

6. This assignment is (harder, more hard) than yesterday's was.

7. The (best, more best) meals are those roasted above an open fire.

8. I was the (least excited, excited) of all my friends about going to the water park.

9. That batch of applesauce is (sweeter, more sweeter) than this batch.

10. Your head is (most protected, more protect) with a bike helmet.

Name _____

Predicate Adjectives

A **predicate adjective** modifies or describes a noun or pronoun like other adjectives, but it must follow a linking verb in a sentence.

Examples: This cake is *good*. (*good* describes *cake*)

Her hair looks *shiny*. (*shiny* describes *hair*)

Underline the predicate adjective in each sentence. Draw an arrow to the noun or pronoun that it modifies.

1. The cookies smell delicious.

2. You look happy.

3. Matt is sick today.

4. The bananas are ripe.

5. His party was fun!

6. The alarm sounds loud.

7. The air became cool after the storm.

8. Lena's bag is heavy!

Articles

A, *an,* and *the* are special adjectives called **articles**.

Use *a* to describe any singular noun that begins with a consonant sound.
    Example: a teacher

Use *an* to describe any singular noun that begins with a vowel sound.
    Example: an analyst

Use *the* with singular or plural nouns to tell about a particular person, place, or thing.
    Example: the typist

Write *a* or *an* in front of each singular noun. Write *the* in front of each plural noun.

1. _____ employee

2. _____ doctor

3. _____ professional

4. _____ actress

5. _____ monarchs

6. _____ candidates

7. _____ designer

8. _____ official

9. _____ architect

10. _____ rangers

11. _____ troopers

12. _____ musicians

13. _____ forester

14. _____ operator

15. _____ gymnast

16. _____ instructors

Articles

Use the articles *a* and *an* correctly with the phrases below.

1. _____ cave explorer

2. _____ impressive cobbler

3. _____ nuclear engineer

4. _____ excited salesperson

5. _____ accomplished writer

6. _____ professional artist

7. _____ radio announcer

8. _____ remarkable ecologist

9. _____ outstanding poet

10. _____ brave astronaut

11. _____ angry bee

12. _____ good friend

13. _____ funny movie

14. _____ incredible game

15. _____ soft blanket

Appositives

An **appositive** is a noun, pronoun, or phrase that identifies or renames the noun or pronoun it follows.

Use a comma before and after an appositive.
    Example: My younger brother's gift, *a blue and orange skateboard*, is exactly what he wanted.

If the noun being explained is too general without the appositive, the information is considered essential and should not be set off with commas.
    Example: The former U.S. president *Theodore Roosevelt* is famous for creating many national parks and monuments.

Circle the appositive in each sentence. Draw an arrow to the noun it identifies or renames.

1. The actor Paul Newman directed only one motion picture.

2. My daughter-in-law, the new sheriff, comes to our house for lunch every Thursday.

3. Uncle Bill liked to ask my mother, his sister, about her new cooking ideas.

Write commas in each sentence where appropriate. Then, circle the appositive in each sentence.

4. It was great having my neighbors Amy and Beth come to my house for dinner.

5. We saw a film clip about President Jimmy Carter on *60 Minutes* the highly acclaimed news program.

6. The new musician Jacob White was an inspiration to younger students.

Write a sentence about a member of your family in which you use an appositive.

_____

_____

_____

Adverbs

> An **adverb** is a word that describes a verb or an adjective.
> Adverbs answer *Where? When? How often? How?* or *To what extent?*
> Example: Please speak *quietly* in the library.

Complete each sentence with an adverb from the box. Use each word once.

truthfully	never	early	quickly
tomorrow	loudly	quietly	excitedly

1. The witness answered the question _____.

2. We ran _____ to get out of the rain.

3. She arrived at the movie 10 minutes _____.

4. We spoke _____ while the baby was sleeping.

5. Can you come over to my house _____?

6. I _____ stay up after 9:00 P.M. on school nights.

7. She cried _____ when she broke her arm.

8. Anna _____ opened her birthday present.

Time Adverbs

A time adverb answers *When?* or *How often?*

Examples: before, continuously, early, eventually, finally, first, frequently, immediately, last night, lately, never, nightly, now, often, once, periodically, rarely, sometimes, soon, then, today, tonight, tomorrow, usually

Complete each sentence with a time adverb. Use an adverb only once.

Brett

Brett _____ loses his glasses. They are _____ found in odd places. His glasses are _____ found on the drinking fountain. He even left them on the soccer field _____. Brett's puppy found his glasses _____. After playing with them for a while, the puppy brought the glasses to Brett _____. Brett promised his mom _____ to leave his glasses lying around again.

Sylvia

Sylvia _____ is awake and attentive. However, she is very tired _____. Sylvia did not get much sleep _____. Her baby brother is sick and cried _____. Sylvia _____ drifted off to sleep. Hopefully, she and her brother will both sleep better _____.

Place Adverbs

A place adverb answers *Where?*
> Examples: anywhere, here, down, there, upstairs, underground, everywhere, away

Circle the place adverbs in each sentence. There may be more than one adverb in a sentence.

1. Many crawly things live outside.

2. I like them better there than inside.

3. They seem to be everywhere you look.

4. They are below, above, and beside you.

5. Ants congregate underground.

6. Worms live there too.

7. Mosquitoes seem to be anywhere people are.

8. One buzzed close to my ear the other day.

9. It seems insects are always nearby.

10. Dragonflies like to hover overhead.

11. Caterpillars sometimes crawl inside a tree trunk.

12. I know insects are helpful to nature, but I would not mind if they stayed far from me!

Manner Adverbs

A **manner adverb** answers *How?* or *In what manner?* Some manner adverbs end in *ly*.

Examples: closely, well, cheerfully, fast, slowly, happily, calmly, bravely, kindly, safely, perfectly, softly, hourly, joyously

Circle the manner adverb in each sentence.

1. The kitten and puppy playfully ran from one end of the room to the other.

2. Jolene's foot tapped nervously.

3. Liza smiled confidently as she stood at the free-throw line.

4. The children waited expectantly for the movie to begin.

5. The fireworks exploded brightly in the night sky.

6. Louis likes to read aloud to the kindergartners.

7. Amber and I walked together to soccer practice.

8. We were completely surprised by the announcement.

9. Owen worked diligently to finish his project by Friday.

10. Quincy carefully climbed the maple tree to get the kite down.

11. Ian quickly rode his bike home in order to meet his curfew.

12. Maddie intently watched the ants carry food crumbs into the anthill.

13. Dakota gently took the artwork off the wall.

14. Ava's mom immediately drenched the fire with water.

Comparative and Superlative Adverbs

> A **comparative adverb** compares two verbs. Usually, a comparative adverb is formed by adding *er* to an adverb.
>
> Example: fast ⟶ faster
>
> A **superlative adverb** compares more than two verbs. Usually, a superlative adverb is formed by adding *est* to an adverb.
>
> Example: fast ⟶ fastest
>
> Add the word *more* or *less* before adverbs ending in *ly* to compare two verbs.
>
> Example: more carefully
>
> Add the word *most* or *least* before adverbs ending in *ly* when comparing more than two verbs.
>
> Example: most carefully
>
> Some comparative and superlative adverbs have irregular spellings.
>
> Example: far ⟶ farther ⟶ farthest

Complete the chart with adverbs that compare the actions of verbs.

Adverbs	Comparative	Superlative
1. completely	_____	_____
2. fondly	_____	_____
3. near	_____	_____
4. wearily	_____	_____
5. close	_____	_____
6. brilliantly	_____	_____
7. timely	_____	_____
8. seriously	_____	_____

Comparative and Superlative Adverbs

Complete each sentence with the correct adverb in parentheses.

1. Clark ran his campaign for our student council president _____ than his opponents. (more successfully, most successfully)

2. He made speeches _____ than his opponents. (most often, more often)

3. Of all the candidates, Clark spoke _____ about his plans for the student government. (more clearly, most clearly)

4. Clark listened _____ than his opponents to the ideas and concerns of his classmates. (more carefully, most carefully)

5. When the teachers announced the winner, the principal clapped the _____. She was his mom! (more loudly, most loudly)

6. Clark smiled _____ than anyone else in the room. (most broadly, more broadly)

Capitalization

Capitalize the first word of every sentence.
    Example: *We* really should go to the game.

Capitalize the first word in a quotation.
    Example: Marnie said, *"You* need help!"

Capitalize all proper nouns.
    Example: *Justin* currently lives in *Des Moines, Iowa.*

Capitalize all proper adjectives.
    Example: Ruth is a *Canadian* citizen.

Circle the words in each sentence that should be capitalized.

1. "and so, my fellow americans," said john f. kennedy, "ask not what your country can do for you, ask what you can do for your country."

2. sara and rachel were excited to go to the dance at roosevelt elementary school.

3. senators and representatives together are called the congress.

4. if tonya wants to come, my mom can pick her up.

5. the south american continent is south of the united states and mexico.

6. since we don't have to go to school on columbus day, I plan to go to manhattan beach with ginger.

7. i've always said, "do to your neighbors as you would have them do to you."

8. people from all over the world come to the taj mahal every year from faraway places such as japan, canada, and australia.

9. if you think you have time to go to barton creek grocery, please buy some milk.

10. galileo was an astronomer and physicist from italy.

Capitalization

Capitalize a person's title when it comes before a name.
Example: *Governor* Jones said that she would veto the new bill.

Capitalize the abbreviations of titles.
Example: *Lt.* Elliott was early for her appointment this morning.

Capitalize the first letter in the abbreviations of days and months, and both letters in the abbreviations for states.
Examples: *AK, CA, VT, Mon., Wed., Feb., Aug.*

Capitalize the first, last, and all other important words in the titles of books, movies, stories, songs, and poems.
Examples: *War* and *Peace*, "*Over* the *Rainbow*"

Circle the words in each sentence that should be capitalized. Refer to the capitalization rules in the previous activity, if necessary.

1. when principal walton came into the room, everyone stopped talking.

2. I hope mr. lipson asks us to read "remember me to harold square" this year.

3. candice arrived on january 1 and left on march 15.

4. at thirteen, sam houston moved from virginia to tennessee.

5. the address on the letter read "georgetown, tx."

6. jessica took her dog, mittens, for a long walk around randolph lake.

7. my granddad said, "your grandma and I are glad you came to visit."

8. the arizona film festival featured a film called "the clay bird."

9. mother's day is always on a sunday.

10. if you see the movie "the wizard of oz," let me know what you think.

Capitalization

Capitalize the first word following a colon when the colon introduces two or more complete sentences.

Example: Drew stated the following reasons why he wasn't joining the basketball league: *First,* he didn't have time. *Second,* he had hurt his ankle. *Third,* he liked soccer better.

Capitalize the first word in the greeting and closing of a letter.

Examples: *Dear* Ms. Robinson,

Yours truly,

Capitalize the names of special events and awards.

Example: The 2004 *Olympic Games* were exciting.

Circle the words in each phrase or sentence that should be capitalized.

1. groundhog day is observed every year on february 2.

2. occasionally, I eat yogurt for breakfast.

3. he attended the national library conference with two friends.

4. best wishes, joe marshall

5. ronnie squire was recently named sheriff of hancock county.

6. helen's dog barks at everything that passes by 4123 inverness road.

7. we have aunt ida to thank for these lovely spring wildflowers.

8. did you know that the same person won the world figure skating championship four different times?

Write a sentence that has at least three capitalized words.

_____

_____

Commas

> The primary purpose of a **comma** (,) is to prevent misunderstandings. Overuse of commas can make reading more difficult.
>
> Use a comma between words or groups of words in a series.
> Example: You should take a cap, gloves, and sunglasses to the slopes.
>
> Use a comma before a conjunction that separates independent clauses.
> Example: Randy wrote the words, and Beth wrote the music.
>
> Use a comma to set off a quotation from the rest of the sentence.
> Example: Amy said, "Remember your jacket!"
>
> Use a comma to set off words in a direct address.
> Example: Look out, Mila, it's coming your way.
>
> Use a comma to separate months and days from years (but not months from years).
> Example: The date was October 12, 1492.
>
> Use a comma to set off an appositive.
> Example: Michael, Katie's older brother, was just hired by my company.

Write commas in each sentence where they are needed.

1. Gretchen can you give me a hand?

2. The mural was filled with splashes of blue green gold and red.

3. Mrs. Jackson my fourth-grade teacher was always my favorite.

4. You can either come to my house or I will come to yours.

5. The campers made sure they brought enough food blankets and water.

6. "Please show me the way out of here" said Mia.

7. I want to leave but I am afraid I will miss something.

8. On Saturday April 18 2005 I went swimming in Crystal Creek.

Name ____

Commas

Use a comma after the greeting in a friendly letter.

Example: Dear Mom,

Use a comma in the closing of a letter.

Example: Sincerely,

Use a comma to separate an ordinal number from the rest of the sentence if it is not used as an adjective.

Example: First, you must turn on the computer.

Use a comma to separate an introductory word or group of words from the rest of the sentence.

Example: Without regret, Jason went to see his old adversary.

Use a comma to separate two or more adjectives modifying the same noun if the word *and* could be inserted between the words without changing the meaning.

Example: Jenny is a careful, honest writer.

Write commas in each phrase or sentence where they are needed.

1. Dear Andy Thank you for coming to play.
2. Fortunately I have already submitted your application.
3. There are benefits to living in a hot dry climate.
4. She is supposed to move into her new house on June 14 2009.
5. Truly yours Abigail
6. My mother's advice was "If you can't say something nice don't say anything at all."
7. I've been thinking a lot about you and I wish you a speedy recovery.
8. Dr. Randolph Damon's father was our troop leader.

Hyphens and Dashes

Use a hyphen (-) when writing out compound numbers from 21 to 99.
   Example: sixty-three

Use a hyphen between compound adjectives that come before the noun they modify.
   Example: French-speaking Canadians

Use a hyphen to separate the syllables of a word that is carried over from one line to the next.
   Example: We went to the movie and then decided to go to a near-
   by delicatessen for a snack.

Use an *en* dash (–) to show a range of dates, times, or reference numbers.
   Example: July–August 2000
                  1:00 P.M.–3:30 P.M.

Use an *em* dash (—) for emphasis.
   Example: When I grow up—which seems like it will take forever—I want to play a professional sport.

Write hyphens and dashes in each sentence where they are needed. Write *H* after the sentence if you used a hyphen, and write *D* if you used a dash.

1. The sports loving fans did not seem to notice the freezing temperature. _____

2. The book focused on the post Civil War period. _____

3. The appointments available are 12:00 P.M. 4:00 P.M. _____

4. The assignment for tomorrow is to read pages 24 36 carefully. Make certain that you read them because there will be a quiz. _____

5. Forty four electric fans are in stock. _____

6. The Chicago New York flight lasts less than two hours. _____

7. We go to great lengths   often far beyond our normal limitations   to win! _____

8. If I only needed to read chapters 2 4, I would be finished by now. _____

Quotation Marks

Use quotation marks (" ") to set off titles of songs, poems, and stories within a collection of other stories.

    Examples: "The Star-Spangled Banner" (song)

              "A Good Walk Spoiled" (poem)

              "The Ugly Duckling" (story within a collection of other stories)

Use quotation marks before and after a direct quote.

    Example: "There's the bus!" yelled Jon.

If the name of the speaker interrupts the quote, place quotation marks before and after the spoken words. The second part of the quote begins with a lowercase letter if it is a continuation of the first part.

    Example: "I am really tired," sighed Becca, "because that race was longer than I thought."

Do not use quotation marks with indirect quotes, which tell what someone said but do not use the person's exact words.

    Example: Mr. Bentley said that he thought we did a good job.

Write quotation marks in each sentence where they are needed.

1. Once out of the storm, Jason shouted, Hurray! We made it!

2. Have you ever been a part of any sports team at your school? asked Silvia.

3. After you take out the trash, said my dad, we can go see a movie.

4. Reid told Angie that Casey at the Bat was one of her favorite poems.

5. Many people have suggested that we adopt the song America the Beautiful as our national anthem.

6. Look out for that bump in the road! shouted Dad.

Name _____

Single Quotation Marks

When a quoted word or a title is used inside a direct quote, single quotation marks are used.

Example: Chelsea said, "I can't seem to spell the word 'peninsula' correctly in this paper."

At the end of a quote, the end punctuation comes between the single and double quotation marks.

Example: "Why can't I spell 'peninsula'?" asked Chelsea.

Rewrite each sentence correctly. Add single quotation marks where needed.

1. Filipe said, "I read the article Bike Safety by Mike B. Helmet."

_____

2. "Would you play America the Beautiful on the piano?" asked Sadie.

_____

3. "My essay Life in Antarctica is due tomorrow," explained Ramsey.

_____

4. "How do you spell beluga?" questioned Maja.

_____

5. "We have to read the chapter Nighttime again," Merle complained.

_____

6. John told Cindy, "Mom said, You certainly may, when I asked her."

_____

7. Mr. Rich announced, "We will sing the song Spring Day."

_____

Apostrophes

> Use an apostrophe (') in a contraction to show where a letter or letters have been omitted.
>
> Example: Since Andy *wasn't* at home, I *didn't* get to see his new home entertainment center.
>
> Use an apostrophe to show ownership or possession.
>
> Example: *Patti's* camera was lying on the backseat of *Mom's* car.
>
> Use an apostrophe to show the plurals of letters, numbers, and words referred to as words. Years can be written with an apostrophe or without.
>
> Examples: I received two *B's* in my math classes.
> The 1990's were exciting years.

Rewrite each sentence, including apostrophes where they are needed.

1. Phil isnt only a singer; hes also a drummer.

   _____

2. Omars golf clubs didnt arrive, so he borrowed his friends set.

   _____

3. Jamies socks and shoes were found in the gym, so shell need to pick them up from the coachs office.

   _____

4. If I study very hard this semester, Im sure Ill make all As.

   _____

5. I thought that the kite was Noras, but she said that it was her sister-in-laws.

   _____

6. Sherrys science classs project grades included 10 As and 10 Bs.

   _____

Semicolons

The primary purpose of a semicolon (;) is to connect equally important independent clauses that are not joined by *and, but, or, nor, for,* or *yet.*

Example: Carlos is happy that September is here; he has been looking forward to being in class with his friends.

Use semicolons to separate items that include commas.

Example: Samantha is planning to invite Sandy, her best friend; Lisette, her next-door neighbor; and Lillie, her cousin.

Use a semicolon between independent clauses that are joined by connecting words such as *however, for example, that is,* and *in fact.* These words are usually followed by commas.

Example: Kayla's aunt took care of her when she was sick; in fact, she remained at her bedside night and day until she recovered.

Write semicolons and commas in each sentence where needed.

1. Marcy forgot to bring a suitcase Mindy remembered.

2. So far this month, John has traveled to Jackson Mississippi Tallahassee Florida and Nashville Tennessee.

3. Rachel wanted to call her brother on his birthday however she was in an airplane most of the day.

4. Casey looked forward to the weekend his uncle was coming to visit.

5. Jonah's class made lunch for Mr. Burns the custodian Mrs. Fry the head cook and Miss Bookman the librarian.

6. Sometimes we stay late after practice however we leave when the coach goes home.

Name _____

Colons

> Use a colon after the main clause to direct the reader's attention to a list.
>
> Example: Davie's travel kit included these items: shaving cream, a razor, a toothbrush, toothpaste, deodorant, and a comb.
>
> Use a colon to introduce formal quotations.
>
> Example: The speaker closed with these words: "He was there when I needed him, and he became the guiding force in my life."
>
> Use a colon after the greeting in a business letter.
>
> Example: Dear Sir:
>
> Use a colon between the hour and minute when writing a time.
>
> The time is 2:15 P.M.
>
> Do not use a colon immediately after a verb. The colon must be preceded by a full independent clause.
>
> Example: Raymond's report told about the difficulties of people who were French, Swedish, and German.

Write colons in each phrase or sentence where needed.

1. At 3 00 P.M., everyone in class needs to take the following to the auditorium a pencil, an eraser, and a notebook.

2. Dear Dr. Wu

3. These students turned their tests in at the same time Jeremy, Raul, Stephanie, and Shawna.

4. I need a few things for a new recipe corn, tomatoes, onions, black beans, and cilantro.

Write a sentence of your own that includes a formal quotation. The first part of the sentence has been started for you. Remember to add a colon where it is needed.

One of my favorite songs begins with these words:

" _____

_____ "

Parts of a Sentence

Every sentence has two main parts, a subject and a predicate.

The **simple subject** is the noun or pronoun that tells who or what the sentence is about.

Example: The older *boys* helped the younger children.

The **complete subject** includes all of the words that identify and modify the simple subject.

Example: *The older boys* helped the younger children.

The **simple predicate** is the verb or verb phrase that tells something about the subject.

Example: The older boys *helped* the younger children.

The **complete predicate** includes all of the words that modify the simple predicate.

Example: The older boys *helped the younger children.*

Circle the complete subject and underline the complete predicate in each sentence.

1. The robin is considered a sign of spring in the Midwest.

2. The Henderson family just moved into an apartment on the 14th floor.

3. I read about the extra traffic that creates problems during the winter.

4. The U.S. Open is one of the most prestigious tennis tournaments.

5. Each member of the Wildcats team deserves a trophy for his participation and hard work.

6. Some rivers flow in a northern direction.

Simple Subjects

Circle the simple subject in each sentence.

1. The brightest star in the sky was easy to find.

2. Ellen's business did well this year.

3. Someone needs to volunteer to take tickets for the fund-raiser at the door.

4. Meanwhile, Adam thought that he should call his mother.

5. Red, white, and blue ribbon decorated the stage for the celebration.

6. The referee tossed a coin into the air to determine which team would get the ball first.

7. In the United States, another name for the president is commander-in-chief.

8. Fortunately, our tickets were for seats close to the playing field.

9. Sadly, Henry was out sick today.

10. Can you bring your favorite book to school to share with the rest of the class?

Simple Predicates

Circle the simple predicate in each sentence.

1. Cindy, Callie, and Courtney are going to the park.

2. Spot wags his tail enthusiastically.

3. Hailey just gave me a high five.

4. I believe just about everything Miss Campbell says.

5. Some people question who invented baseball.

6. From Pluto, the sun would look much smaller than it looks from Earth.

7. Those elephants are from India, not Africa.

8. A tuna can swim 100 miles in a single day.

9. Bill patiently sat on the bench near the bus stop.

10. We played tag until lunch.

11. Someone in the next room just called my name.

12. Some people say that a plastic container can take as long as 50,000 years to decompose.

Simple Subjects and Predicates

> Sometimes all or part of the predicate comes before the subject. When that happens, the sentence is said to be in **inverted order**.
>
> Example: Near the lake are many boats.
>
> (In this sentence, *boats* is the simple subject and *are* is the simple predicate.)

Circle the simple subject and draw a line under the simple predicate in each sentence. In addition, if a sentence is in inverted order, draw an X through the number of the sentence.

1. Mel went on a vacation to Northern California.

2. I included Robyn's name on the list of the planning committee.

3. Down the middle of Market Street came the parade.

4. Ashley sewed a new button on her jacket.

5. I cannot imagine how we found this place without help from Angie.

6. In the window seat sat the cats.

Write a sentence. Then, circle the simple subject and underline the simple predicate.

_____

_____

Name _____

Complete Subjects and Predicates

Write a complete subject or predicate to complete each sentence.

1. _____ should be enough to fill you up.

2. Our bus ride to Los Angeles, California, _____.

3. The weather for this coming weekend _____.

4. The tallest building downtown _____.

5. _____ brought his dog Bingo to school last Wednesday.

6. _____ placed her award on a shelf.

7. Brittany and her brother Phillip _____.

8. _____ would be a great vacation.

Compound Subjects

A **compound subject** is made up of two or more simple subjects that have the same verb or verb phrase.

Example: Kelly and Tracie loved to play tennis.

Circle the words that make up the compound subject in each sentence.

1. California, Oregon, and Washington have western borders on the Pacific Ocean.

2. Maggie and Carlotta created an award-winning science project on algae.

3. Both Massachusetts and Illinois have cities named Quincy.

4. Orville and Wilbur Wright flipped a coin to decide who would fly.

5. Writing and art are Alvie's favorite subjects.

6. Aunt Gerry and Uncle Floyd come to our house every year on my birthday.

7. Hot dogs and hamburgers are popular foods for American parties.

8. Flag Day, Veterans Day, Memorial Day, and Independence Day are national holidays in the United States.

9. Tacos, burritos, and enchiladas taste great with cheese.

10. England, Spain, and France had interests in the New World.

11. Holly, Wendy, Denise, and Sherry were inseparable friends during middle school.

12. Calvin and Pete became friends during their aerobics class.

Compound Predicates

> A **compound predicate** is made up of two or more separate verbs that have the same subject.
>
> Example: Before going to the game, Matthew finished his homework and ate a healthy dinner.

Circle the words that make up the compound predicate in each sentence.

1. I have saved all of the stories about Marnie's rescue and pasted them into a scrapbook.

2. Charlotte saved her money for two months and then bought a radio for her room.

3. The bluebird population will probably stabilize for a few years and then rise again.

4. Light travels 186,000 miles per second and takes six hours to reach Earth from Pluto.

5. Police fight crime every day and keep our community safe.

6. I can mow the lawn and pick up the grass clippings at the same time with our new lawnmower.

7. Ms. Metcalf gave our class free time today, but she assigned us reading for tomorrow.

8. Karina catches the ball and then brings it back to Halle to play some more.

9. Mom's cookies smelled and tasted great!

10. Kiley ran to the store and returned home in time for her favorite TV show.

11. Jake's dad works as an engineer and coaches our baseball team.

12. Aaron raked the front lawn and then bagged all the leaves.

Compound Subjects and Predicates

The sentences below contain either a compound subject or a compound predicate. Circle the words that make up each compound subject and underline the words that make up each compound predicate.

1. Corn and green beans are my two favorite vegetables.

2. The game both entertained and excited the baseball fans.

3. Beth cooked her dinner and then ate it.

4. Diana and I cooked dinner for her parents.

5. Those attending the school picnic sipped lemonade and played games on the soccer field.

6. Vanilla and butter pecan are my two favorite flavors of ice cream.

Write a sentence about your family that has a compound subject.

_____

_____

Write a sentence about a close friend that has a compound predicate.

_____

_____

Name _____

Subject-Verb Agreement

The subject and verb of a sentence must agree in number.

Singular subjects must have singular verbs. Most verbs are made singular by adding *s* or *es*. *Is, was, has,* and *does* are irregular singular verbs.

Examples: The road *winds* up the mountain.

The road *is* bumpy.

Plural subjects must have plural verbs. *Are, were, have,* and *do* are irregular plural verbs.

Examples: The roads *wind* up the mountain.

The roads *are* bumpy.

Underline the subject of each sentence. Then, circle the correct form of the verb.

1. Some of the beads (is, are) missing from the necklace.

2. Where (is, are) the gate to her house?

3. Tucson (lies, lie) to the south of Phoenix.

4. A statue of Andrew Jackson (stand, stands) in Jackson Square.

5. The Dodgers, Braves, and Cardinals (is, are) division leaders.

Complete each sentence with a verb that makes sense and agrees in number with the subject.

6. Brittany and Mel _____ their homework immediately after school.

7. If the sheep are in the meadow, the cows _____ in the barn.

8. Tourists _____ warmer climates in the winter.

9. Christie _____ much more slowly than Merilee.

10. The home-team fans always _____ more loudly than the away-team fans.

Subject-Verb Agreement

Underline the subject in each sentence. Then, circle the verb that agrees with the subject in number.

1. Gretchen (goes, go) home from college every weekend to see her parents.

2. Carlos and Ben (has been, have been) friends since they were in the third grade.

3. Lindsey (play, plays) on the tennis courts at her apartment building.

4. Both the Yankees and the Mets (calls, call) New York City their home.

5. Trail Ridge Road (winds, wind) its way through Rocky Mountain National Park.

6. The questions on the test (was, were) easy to answer after studying so hard.

7. In the United States, the president and the vice president (runs, run) as a team during a presidential election.

8. Kiley (brings, bring) her pet iguana to school every year for "Pets on Parade Week."

Subject-Verb Agreement

Agreement errors are common when using the contractions *there's,* *here's,* and *where's.*

Examples: Where's the cookies?   (incorrect because *cookies* is plural)

Where's the cookie?   (correct)

Where are the cookies? (correct)

Write a word or pair of words from the box to complete each sentence with the correct subject-verb agreement. You will use some words or pairs more than once.

| Where's | Here's | There's |
| Where are | Here are | There are |

1. _____ my mom.

2. _____ your slippers?

3. _____ your lost dog.

4. _____ the dictionary?

5. _____ some books you might like.

6. _____ drinks on the table.

7. _____ the hospital?

8. _____ my socks?

9. _____ my sister.

10. _____ some tracks.

Prepositions

A **preposition** is a word that shows the relationship between two words in a sentence. It can tell where something is, where something is going, when something happens, or the relationship between a noun or pronoun and another word.

Examples:

about	above	across	after	against
among	at	before	beneath	behind
below	between	beyond	by	down
during	except	for	from	in
inside	into	like	near	of
off	on	out	outside	over
through	to	toward	under	until
up	upon	with	within	without
according to	along with	because of	next to	except for
in addition to	in back of	in front of	in spite of	on account of

When a preposition is used without an object, it becomes an adverb.

Example: Jeff fell *behind* the group of runners. (preposition)

Jeff fell *behind*. (adverb)

Circle the prepositions in each sentence below.

1. Gracie and Helen had not seen each other for 50 years.

2. "Tell me about Grandpa," said Randy.

3. The water packs were carried on their backs.

4. I would go into the garden, but it is muddy.

5. Tommy passed the peas to his mother.

6. We should meet somewhere beyond the city limits.

7. The lights come on automatically after sunset.

8. Please put an umbrella in the trunk.

Prepositional Phrases

A **prepositional phrase** begins with a preposition and ends with a noun or pronoun. The noun or pronoun in a prepositional phrase is called the object of the preposition. A preposition always has an object. If the word does not have an object, it is not acting as a preposition. A sentence can have more than one prepositional phrase.

Example: The book *on* the *desk* is mine.

Preposition: on

Object of the preposition: desk

Prepositional phrase: on the desk

Draw a box around each preposition. Circle each object of the preposition. Underline each prepositional phrase. There may be more than one in a sentence.

1. The mare thundered around the corral.

2. Ellen's sunset photograph is hanging on our living-room wall.

3. Kaela's favorite part of dessert was eating the tip of her ice-cream cone.

4. Jena hugged her horse with all her strength.

5. Gina walked carefully by the edge of the pond.

6. The washed grapes are in the blue bowl.

7. Maddie fell asleep with her plate in her lap.

8. Mr. Tennison has a bag of jelly beans in his desk drawer.

9. The box of books is located behind the door.

10. The jar of homemade strawberry jam did not last long.

11. We are renting the cottage near the dock.

12. Blaine walked up the mountain until he reached the top.

Prepositional Phrases

Underline each prepositional phrase. Circle each object of the preposition. There may be more than one prepositional phrase in each sentence.

1. We were forced to find shelter from the weather.

2. In the afternoon, we drove toward Memphis.

3. Until that point, everything had gone well.

4. Rene used the spare key to his parents' house that was under the birdbath.

5. The new dog in our neighborhood has tags around its neck.

6. My desk is covered with paper junk mail.

7. Dad slept through the whole show.

8. In place of nails, I used screws.

9. There were boulders and rocks beside the bridge.

10. Laura was grateful for Rita's kindness.

Prepositional Phrases

A prepositional phrase can be used to modify a noun, a pronoun, a verb, an adjective, or an adverb.

When a prepositional phrase is used to modify a noun or a pronoun, it is used as an adjective.

Example: Our run *to the beach* was fun.

When a prepositional phrase is used to modify a verb, an adjective, or an adverb, it is used as an adverb.

Example: Wendy dove *into the pool*.

Underline the prepositional phrase in each sentence. Write the word *adjective* or *adverb* to tell how the phrase is used.

1. The papers were organized in alphabetical order. _____

2. She held a glimmer of hope. _____

3. The weeds by the door were brown. _____

4. The tomatoes from our garden were delicious. _____

5. Janie went home with the extra food. _____

6. John hit the ball across the field. _____

7. Sweat was running down her face. _____

8. Please raise the window about halfway. _____

9. Andy found his wallet under his bed. _____

10. The cover of that book is recycled paper. _____

Write a sentence that describes summer. Include at least one prepositional phrase. Underline each prepositional phrase. Write the word *adjective* or *adverb* above each phrase to tell how the phrase is used.

_____

_____

Name _____

Direct Objects

> A **direct object** is the noun or pronoun that receives the action of the verb. It is located in the predicate of a sentence. The predicate is the part of the sentence with a verb.
>
> To locate the direct object, find the verb. Find a noun after the verb that answers *What?* or *Whom?* If the noun is receiving the action of the verb, the noun is the direct object.
>
> Examples: The ball hit *the target*.
>
> I gave Chad *some money*.

Underline the verb in each sentence. Circle the direct objects.

1. The courtyard fountain continuously gushed water.

2. Leona frequently chews gum.

3. The anxious horse kicked the stall door.

4. Erica handed Jacob her paper.

5. Rochelle stowed the luggage in the overhead bin.

6. Danielle offered her carrots to Jesse.

7. Rosa canceled her subscription to the magazine.

8. Yolanda crochets a blue and white blanket.

9. The hot chicken soup burned April's tongue.

10. Enrique toasted a marshmallow over the campfire.

Direct Objects

Circle the direct object in each sentence.

1. Andy arrived at math class on time, but he forgot a pencil.

2. Sherrie always helps decorate the family Christmas tree.

3. Dad grilled the salmon on cedar planks.

4. Kelly swept her room after she had picked up her clothes.

5. Carrie called Gretchen to make plans for Saturday.

6. Jon played his banjo for his family.

7. Many people fear the diamondback rattlesnake.

8. Kerry asked Aaron to play a game with him.

Write one sentence with a direct object and one sentence without a direct object.

_____

_____

_____

_____

Name _____

Indirect Objects

> An **indirect object** is the noun or pronoun that answers *To whom? For whom? To what?* or *For what?* The indirect object is located in the predicate of the sentence and usually comes between the verb and the direct object.
>
> Example: Everett handed *Harry* a dollar.

Underline the verbs in each sentence. Circle the indirect objects.

1. José gave his puppy a bath.

2. Peter wished his grandmother a happy birthday.

3. Walter sold Alan the tire swing.

4. The waiter handed Kent his dinner platter.

5. Quinn offered Tommy her pencil.

6. Aunt May knitted June a new yellow scarf.

7. Mr. Slider gave the chair a coat of varnish.

8. The students wrote a family member a letter.

9. The new neighbor made our family stir-fried vegetables.

10. Roberta saved Rico some sweet corn.

11. Franco sent his friends invitations to his pool party.

12. Allison served her family iced lemonade.

13. Lydia handed Stanton her beach towel.

14. Alex will save Jerome a seat on the bus after school.

Indirect Objects

Circle the indirect object in the following sentences. Write *none* if the sentence does not have an indirect object.

1. I sent my teacher a card.

2. Ms. Johnson surprised everybody in our English class with a pop quiz.

3. Mom gave me $5 for mowing our lawn yesterday.

4. The cashier asked me a question about the coupon.

5. Callie listened to the guest speaker at the library.

6. Mr. Linden showed me a map of the school.

7. Anyone interested in trying out for the volleyball team should tell Coach Olsen.

8. I read my older brother a story that I wrote.

Write one sentence with an indirect object and one sentence without an indirect object.

_____

_____

_____

_____

Name _____

Clauses

A clause is a group of words with a subject and a predicate.

An **independent clause** can stand alone as a sentence.
  Example: Jane plays baseball.

A **dependent clause** cannot stand alone; it is used with an independent clause.
  Example: because she likes the sport

Write *I* if the group of words is an independent clause. Write *D* if the group of words is a dependent clause.

_____ 1. whenever Dillon receives a letter

_____ 2. everyone encourages him

_____ 3. Jasmine rides her horse Tally

_____ 4. so Chad bought a new bat

_____ 5. those flowers are blooming early

_____ 6. until Lila finishes her homework

_____ 7. I walked a mile before school

_____ 8. since it was thundering and lightning

_____ 9. because the box of crackers was unopened

_____10. Kirsten chewed a stick of gum

_____11. the store closed at six o'clock

_____12. if Mark orders dessert

_____13. Lynn hung the picture on the wall

_____14. although the power went out

Relative Clauses

A **relative clause** is a dependent clause that modifies a noun or pronoun and begins with a relative pronoun or relative adverb. *Who, whom, whose, that,* and *which* are relative pronouns. *When, where,* and *why* are relative adverbs.

Examples: That's the one *that I like best.*

Farmers say that spring rains, *which usually begin in April,* are good for the crops.

Relative clauses are set off with commas if they add information to the sentence that is not necessary.

Underline the relative clause in each sentence.

1. The deck was so wet that it was slippery.

2. The story that Ms. Hobbin read was about monsters.

3. Jenny, who is the fastest girl on the track team, is my best friend.

4. The woman who is wearing white shorts is my mom.

5. We went on a vacation, which was relaxing and fun.

6. Please give this dollar to Holly, who is the treasurer of the student council.

7. The audition will be held at the hotel where many participants are staying.

8. Breakfast begins at 7:00 A.M., when the kitchen opens.

Name _____

Independent and Dependent Clauses

Write *I* if the group of words is an independent clause. Write *D* if the group of words is a dependent clause.

_____ 1. Ryan could only bring two

_____ 2. last year he tried to visit New York City

_____ 3. we should not spend time arguing

_____ 4. because Rachel decided she could come

Circle the independent clause and underline the dependent clause in each sentence.

5. Although I can participate, I can't stay long.

6. When Charlie's sister leaves, Charlie plays with his neighbor.

7. She knows more teachers at school because she is older than her brother.

8. Since the road is new, it is perfectly smooth.

Write a sentence that includes both an independent clause and a dependent clause. Circle the independent clause and underline the dependent clause.

_____

_____

_____

Sentence Building with Clauses

Draw a line from each dependent clause to the independent clause that completes the sentence.

Dependent clause	Independent clause
1. if you save your money.	Toto got a treat
2. Because the leaves were changing colors	Jonah's stepdad took him to school.
3. When I see the street sign,	I know the movie is good.
4. From the large crowd of people,	we knew autumn was here.
5. Since his mother was sick,	You can buy a new video game
6. because he is a good dog.	I know to turn right.
7. The game was exciting,	I'm looking forward to the event,
8. which will be held on Saturday morning.	but I had to leave early.

9. Write a dependent clause.

_____

10. Now add an independent clause to the dependent clause to make a sentence.

_____

Conjunctions

A **conjunction** is a word that is used to join words or groups of words.

Coordinating conjunctions connect words, phrases, and clauses that are related.

    Examples: and, or, but, for, nor, yet, so

Correlative conjunctions are used in pairs to connect words, phrases, and clauses and explain their relationship to each other.

    Examples: either...or

                 neither...nor

                 not only...but also

                 both...and

Subordinating conjunctions come at the beginning of a dependent clause and establish the clause's relationship to the independent clause.

    Examples: after, although, since, when, if

Circle the conjunctions in each sentence. Then, write the type of conjunction.

1. Although Ben likes soccer best, he plays baseball too. _____

2. Ramond is good at both math and science. _____

3. Amy liked the new ending she wrote for the story, but she was considering changing it again.

   _____

4. Since Ethan is captain of the team, he made a spirit banner for the game. _____

5. Ms. Carlson has five gardens, yet all of them have only roses. _____

6. We can go to either a museum or an art gallery to see modern paintings. _____

7. Mary Lynn plays not only the piano but also the saxophone. _____

8. We saw both Angel and Nancy on the running track. _____

Coordinating Conjunctions

Combine each set of sentences using a coordinating conjunction from the box. Write the new sentence on the line. Use each coordinating conjunction once.

and	or	but	for	yet	so

1. Devin went swimming in the pool. He did not go swimming in the lake.

   _____

   _____

2. She enjoys making art. She chooses to spend more time playing sports.

   _____

   _____

3. Josie picked up her backpack. She got on the bus.

   _____

   _____

4. We can watch the movie. We can meet Joe at the park.

   _____

   _____

5. The apples are not mine. I don't know if you can have one.

   _____

   _____

6. Craig likes riding in airplanes. It makes him feel like he is a bird.

   _____

   _____

Correlative Conjunctions

Circle the correlative conjunctions in each sentence.

1. Last night both Trey and Noreen won awards.

2. Just as cars follow street signs, so must bikes.

3. Neither the map nor the itinerary fit in Ophelia's scrapbook.

4. We could use either molasses or sugar to sweeten the cookies.

5. Bea not only decorated the cupcakes but also made them from scratch.

6. Neither Carlos nor Mirabel is going to the meeting tonight.

7. Either a period or a semicolon can separate a run-on sentence.

8. Whether it rains or not, we will play soccer.

9. Both the paper and the project are due on Friday.

10. Mr. Oliver said that I can either bring my own pencil or borrow one.

11. June wants both salt and pepper on her vegetables.

12. You need to wear not only protective eyeglasses but also a helmet.

Subordinating Conjunctions

Write *I* if the group of words is an independent clause. Write *D* if the group of words is a dependent clause. Circle the subordinating conjunction in each dependent clause.

_____ 1. since I first graduated from college

_____ 2. Ginny is a really good person

_____ 3. after the storm had ended

_____ 4. few could climb the mountain

_____ 5. when the floodwaters had subsided

_____ 6. because she, too, lost her camping gear

_____ 7. the victory dance has already begun

_____ 8. when Chris cheers loudly for the basketball team

_____ 9. since the rules haven't been followed at all so far

_____10. they were all very nervous

Write a sentence that begins with a subordinating conjunction.

_____

_____

Building Sentences

Write three sentences. Then, follow the directions for each sentence.

1. Draw a line between the complete subject and the complete predicate.

2. Underline the simple subject.

3. Circle the verb.

4. Write D.O. over the direct object, if there is one.

5. Write I.O. over the indirect object, if there is one.

6. Put a box around each prepositional phrase.

1. _____

_____

_____

2. _____

_____

_____

3. _____

_____

_____

Expanding Sentences

Sentences can be improved by adding details that will make them more specific and interesting. Details in sentences can answer such questions as *When? Where? What kind? Which one? How often?* and *To what degree?*

   Example: The ball left the park. ⟶ The towering fly ball was still rising as it went over the fence and left the ballpark.

Expand each of the sentences by adding details that will help answer some of the above questions.

1. The rock broke her window. _____

_____

2. The woman walked down the street. _____

_____

3. The fire truck responded. _____

_____

4. The basement was flooded. _____

_____

5. My cousin bought a car. _____

_____

6. My stepdad made dinner. _____

_____

7. Susan is nice. _____

_____

Types of Sentences

A **declarative sentence** makes a statement or states a fact and ends with a period.

Example: Many have followed the rocky road to success.

An **interrogative sentence** asks a question and ends with a question mark.

Example: Would you go to the store with me?

An **imperative sentence** gives a command or makes a request and ends with a period.

Example: Deliver this note to Mrs. Carmen.

An **exclamatory sentence** expresses a strong feeling and ends with an exclamation point.

Example: What a great day to go to the beach!

Write *D* in front of each declarative sentence, *INT* in front of each interrogative sentence, *IMP* in front of each imperative sentence, and *E* in front of each exclamatory sentence. Then, place the correct punctuation mark at the end of each sentence.

_____ 1. Living in this city is so exciting____

_____ 2. Please repeat what you said earlier____

_____ 3. What an amazing performance James gave____

_____ 4. Jeff started playing golf at a young age____

_____ 5. Will you pass the peas, please____

_____ 6. Lay your pencil down when you are finished____

_____ 7. Did you get to see Will's performance____

_____ 8. I love my baby sister so much____

_____ 9. Logan sent an invitation to Anna through e-mail____

_____10. What a beautiful ship it was____

_____11. Will you give me a helping hand____

_____12. I am so glad you are coming to my concert____

Types of Sentences

Write the correct punctuation mark at the end of each sentence.

1. Which of these sentences is correct___

2. Sarah's motivation was clear___

3. The price of rice is consistent___

4. Shake it off___

5. If I go, will you come with me___

6. Rutherford B. Hayes won one of the most hotly contested presidential races in U.S. history___

7. Your shirt is a nice color___

8. As they say in show business, "Break a leg___"

9. The waves on the lake are high today___

10. I can't believe my ears___

Run-On Sentences

A **run-on sentence** occurs when two or more sentences are run together without proper punctuation.

Example: I like the way you draw, I like the colors you use in your paintings.

A run-on sentence can be corrected by separating it into two sentences or by separating the two clauses with a semicolon or a comma and a conjunction.

Example: I like the way you draw. I like the colors you use in your paintings.

Example: I like the way you draw, and I like the colors you use in your paintings.

Example: I like the way you draw; I like the colors you use in your paintings.

Correct each run-on sentence.

1. My house is near a market I can walk to get a sandwich.

   _____

   _____

2. The man who makes the sandwiches is named Dan he is really nice he gives me extra pickles.

   _____

   _____

3. Sometimes I ride my bike instead of walking I can get there faster I can carry groceries in my basket.

   _____

   _____

4. On the way home from the market, I start nibbling on fresh vegetables that are grown by local farmers who brought them to the market to sell and if you get there early enough you can see them unloading their trucks.

   _____

   _____

Name _____

Sentence Fragments

Remember, a complete sentence requires both a subject and a predicate. A **sentence fragment** is an incomplete sentence, or a sentence without a subject or a predicate.

Examples: Played a great match but lost. (no subject)

Samantha, my sister. (no predicate)

Write *C* on the line if the group of words is a complete sentence. Write *F* on the line if the group of words is a sentence fragment.

_____ 1. I plan to be there before anyone else.

_____ 2. If you go camping, be certain you take a warm sleeping bag.

_____ 3. Behind the barn.

_____ 4. When the game ended.

_____ 5. The jockey mounted his horse.

_____ 6. Whether there is enough food or not.

_____ 7. Swimming in the lake.

_____ 8. The concert ended too soon.

Rewrite each of these sentence fragments as complete sentences.

9. From high atop the stadium.

_____

_____

10. Hidden under the basket.

_____

_____

Active and Passive Voice

In the **active voice**, the subject is doing the action.

Example: Todd fixed Mrs. Horvath's window.

In the **passive voice**, the subject is being acted upon.

Example: Mrs. Horvath's window was fixed by Todd.

Rewrite each sentence that is in the active voice into the passive voice. Rewrite each sentence that is in the passive voice into the active voice.

1. Experiments have been conducted by students to test the hypothesis.

_____

2. Over two-thirds of the applicants passed the exam.

_____

3. The results of the research will be published in the next issue of the journal.

_____

_____

4. The school secretary notified the teacher that one student was absent.

_____

_____

5. The vegetarian pizza was enjoyed by all of my friends.

_____

6. Tim hammered the nail into the timber.

_____

Double Negatives

Negatives are words that usually begin with the letter *n*; *no, none, not, nobody, nothing, never, neither,* and *no one* are examples of negatives.

Proper grammar usage of a negative word avoids the use of two in the same sentence.

    Example: I do not want nothing in this bag except groceries!   (incorrect)

          I do not want anything in this bag except groceries!   (correct)

However, if a comma follows a negative, it is acceptable to use another negative in the same sentence.

    Example: No, Shannon does not want to go to the park today.

Some negatives that do not begin with the letter *n* include *scarcely, hardly,* and *barely.*

Rewrite each sentence to correct the double negatives.

1. Sidney couldn't do nothing with her hair.

   _____

2. Todd didn't have no second thoughts about the decision he made.

   _____

3. No, Celia didn't see nobody else at the market.

   _____

4. Kevin could not barely see the road because of the heavy snow.

   _____

5. Mia hasn't received no mail in more than a week.

   _____

6. Parker wasn't planning no visit to California in the near future.

   _____

Name _____

Doesn't and *Don't*

> *Doesn't* is the contraction of *does not*. It should be used with singular nouns and the pronouns *he, she,* and *it*.
>
>   Example: Madeline doesn't want to go.
>
> *Don't* is the contraction of *do not*. It should be used with plural nouns and the pronouns *I, you, we,* and *they*.
>
>   Example: The students in Ms. Li's class don't all get out at 3:00 P.M.

Circle the correct contraction in each sentence.

1. Why (doesn't, don't) Cassie ever arrive on time?

2. It (doesn't, don't) happen very often.

3. Terry and I (doesn't, don't) think it will rain today.

4. This math problem (doesn't, don't) fit with the others.

5. This battery (doesn't, don't) work.

6. Becca and Royce (doesn't, don't) want to eat too late.

7. Why (doesn't, don't) you and your friend carpool?

8. Gordon (doesn't, don't) like the idea of putting ketchup on eggs.

9. Golfers (doesn't, don't) play when it is stormy.

10. My rabbit (doesn't, don't) like to eat celery.

11. This nail (doesn't, don't) work for hanging that picture.

12. Romero and Holly (doesn't, don't) care much for dessert.

Who and *Whom*

Use *who* as a subject pronoun. *Whoever* can also be used as a subject.

　　Examples: *Who* came to the graduation party?

　　　　　　Whoever needs extra help can see me after class.

Use *whom* as an object pronoun. *Whomever* can also be used as an object pronoun.

　　Examples: *Whom* did you bring home for dinner?

　　　　　　The trophy is for *whomever* the judges select.

Use *whom* as the object of a preposition.

　　Example: To *whom* do you wish me to give this message?

Write either *who* or *whom* to complete each sentence.

1. _____ made the first moon landing?

2. _____ do you like the best among the candidates?

3. _____ is your very best friend in the whole world?

4. _____ won the gold medal?

5. _____ does Ryan think will be the best choice for the math contest?

6. _____ was the man she saw walking his dog?

7. _____ shall I call in case of an emergency?

8. He is the person _____ is always late!

9. One of the boys _____ we know is very tall.

10. A teacher _____ we admire spoke at our graduation.

Write a sentence of your own in which you use either *who* or *whom* correctly.

_____

Lie/Lay and *May/Can*

Lie means "to recline" and does not take a direct object.
> Example: Why won't you *lie* down and rest?

Lay means "to place" and does take a direct object.
> Example: When will they *lay* your new carpet?

Use *may* to ask permission.
> Example: *May* I have a piece of that pizza?

Use *can* to express the ability to do something.
> Example: Phil *can* play golf very well.

Circle the correct choice for each of the following.

1. Bingo, (lie, lay) down!

2. Toto (may, can) do several tricks if you give him a reward for his actions.

3. Mom, (may, can) Amy spend the night on Friday?

4. No one (may, can) understand the problem like Evelyn!

5. Janie (may, can) return to work when she is feeling well again.

6. If you see Mandy, you (may, can) offer her a ride home.

7. Please (lie, lay) the paper on the stairs.

8. You may (lie, lay) the magazine on the table when you're finished looking at it.

9. I (may, can) only reach the green if I hit the ball a long way!

10. The cat wants to (lie, lay) down on the blanket.

Write a sentence that includes the word *lie*.

_____

Write a sentence that includes the word *lay*.

_____

That and *Which*

> The pronouns *that* and *which* can help you decide if you need commas.
>
> Use *that* and no comma when the modifier is necessary for meaning. Such clauses that are necessary to define the meaning are called restrictive clauses and do not require commas.
>
>   Example: Circle the answer that best answers each question.
>
> Use *which* and a comma or commas when the modifier is not necessary for meaning. Such clauses are called nonrestrictive clauses and require commas.
>
>   Example: The temperature, which is normal for this time of year, is in the high 80s.

Circle the correct word, *that* or *which*, for each sentence.

1. Sarah rode the bicycle (that, which) belonged to her brother.

2. Bicycles, (that, which) are relatively inexpensive, provide transportation and exercise.

3. The band (that, which) will perform first tonight is from Kansas City, Missouri.

4. The flute (that, which) Jerry accidentally dropped cannot be fixed by this evening.

5. Babe Ruth's home-run record, (that, which) now has been broken several times, stood for over three decades.

6. I am looking for a magazine (that, which) reviews new songs.

Write a sentence using *that*.

_____

Write a sentence using *which*.

_____

Synonyms and Antonyms

A **synonym** is a word that has the same or nearly the same meaning as another word.

Examples: earth = soil

away = absent

An **antonym** is a word that has the opposite meaning of another word.

Examples: tall ≠ short

happy ≠ sad

Write a synonym for the underlined word in each sentence.

1. When you launder your clothes, be certain to use soap. _____

2. Winning the lottery was exciting for Matthew. _____

3. The winter day was dreary. _____

Write a synonym for each of the following words.

4. gather _____   7. quickly _____

5. jump _____   8. tired _____

6. crawl _____   9. sprint _____

Write an antonym for the underlined word in each sentence.

10. The morning rush-hour traffic created a real mess! _____

11. With camera in hand, the photographer was there to capture the beautiful sunset.

_____

12. I can't imagine a more difficult dilemma. _____

Write an antonym for each of the following words.

13. straight _____   16. horrible _____

14. narrow _____   17. open _____

15. near _____   18. find _____

Homophones and Homographs

A **homophone** is a word that sounds the same as another word but has a different spelling and a different meaning.

> Examples: pail, pale
>
> know, no

A **homograph** is a word that has the exact same spelling as another word but has a different meaning and sometimes has a different pronunciation.

> Example: bank: a place where people keep their money
>
> bank: the land along the sides of a river

Circle the correct homophone or homophones to complete each sentence.

1. Tanya (new, knew) how to get along with (new, knew) people she met.

2. The (our, hour) hand on (our, hour) new clock doesn't move correctly.

3. I like to (read, reed) magazines about sports.

4. You can (buy, by) a good used TV in the store next (to, two, too) the shopping mall.

5. Spencer and Jack invited me to come to (there, their) house after school.

6. Mrs. Brinks told her students to bring (to, two, too) pencils to class for the test.

7. I (see, sea) a beautiful sunset down by the (see, sea) every night.

8. Our cat, Cosby, sometimes chases his (tale, tail).

Use one of the homographs from the box to complete each sentence.

vault	checks	safe	interest

9. Raul was _____ at second base.

10. Mr. Beamon _____ our assignments every day for errors.

11. Rae Ann uses a long pole to _____ over the bar.

12. The critic looked at the new painting with great _____.

Synonyms, Antonyms, Homonyms, and Homographs

If the underlined words in each sentence are synonyms, write *S*. If they are antonyms, write *A*. If they are homophones, write *HP*. If they are homographs, write *HG*.

_____ 1. The wind <u>blew</u> the puffy clouds across the <u>blue</u> sky.

_____ 2. I can't <u>lie</u>; it's impossible for my dog to <u>lie</u> still.

_____ 3. It was <u>unknown</u> who won the <u>famous</u> tournament.

_____ 4. Tonya will <u>pursue</u> a degree in biology, but first she must <u>seek</u> a college loan.

_____ 5. To <u>squeeze</u> the orange well, you have to <u>compress</u> the clamp all the way.

_____ 6. As J. J. <u>read</u> the book, he noticed a <u>red</u> spot on the page.

_____ 7. Everything will be <u>fine</u>, even if I have to pay a <u>fine</u>.

_____ 8. The flowers are so <u>beautiful</u>, but the weeds are <u>ugly</u>!

_____ 9. The <u>rigid</u> piece of wood made the position of the table's leg <u>unalterable</u>.

_____10. I thought I could detect a slight <u>smile</u> behind the <u>frown</u> on Mindy's face.

Name _____

Idioms

An **idiom** is an expression that has a meaning different from the usual meanings of the words within the expression.

Example: to fly off the handle = to lose control of one's temper

Underline each idiom. Then, write what you think it means.

1. The city council was on the fence about building the new city hall.

_____

2. Mr. Banks was commenting on the nice weather, when it began to rain out of the blue.

_____

3. Maya was out of sight, out of mind; Randy soon forgot all about her.

_____

4. Sam was on pins and needles waiting for the results from the election.

_____

5. Liz knew that a penny saved is a penny earned, so she always cooked lunch at home instead of eating out.

_____

6. Andy went the extra mile; he learned the entire poem instead of just one stanza.

_____

Write a sentence using an idiom you have heard.

_____

_____

Business Letters

Business letters have seven parts: return address, date, inside address, greeting, body, closing, and signature.

The **return address** is the writer's address. It includes the writer's name, street address, city, state, and zip code.

The **date** appears directly below the return address.

The **inside address** includes the name of the person to whom the letter is being written, his or her company name, and the street address, city, state, and zip code.

The **greeting** is a formal beginning to the letter and includes the person's title and last name followed by a colon.

The **body** is the main content of the letter.

The **closing** is a formal end to the letter. *Sincerely* is an appropriate closing.

The **signature** is the writer's full name and comes at the end of the letter.

Label the parts of the business letter.

Miss Patricia Boyd
243 Oak Avenue
Thisplace, Ohio 12345 _____

Monday, October 3, 2010 _____

Mrs. G. H. Wells
Chamber of Commerce
33 Icy Avenue
Colder, Alaska 11111 _____

Dear Mrs G. H. Wells: _____

Hello. I am writing this letter to request information about your city. Mr. Smarts, my social studies teacher, said that many chambers of commerce can send information about their towns. I would like any materials you can send, please. _____

Sincerely, _____

Patricia Boyd _____

Business Letters

Write a business letter.

_____

_____

_____

_____

_____

_____

_____

_____

_____

_____

_____

_____

_____

_____

Writing Dialogue

When writing a conversation, begin a new paragraph every time the speaker changes.

Example:

"Mark, did you go to the basketball game yesterday?" asked Eddie.

"Yes, I did," answered Mark.

"Did you see Max make that layup? It was great!"

"You bet," said Mark. "It was one in a million."

Rewrite the following conversation using the appropriate punctuation.

Boy, am I in trouble cried Joan. What's the problem asked Virginia. I left my house key in my room and now I can't get in. Mom won't be home for two more hours, Joan said. Virginia said Let's leave a note on your door, then go to my house. Your mom can pick you up there. Great idea said Joan.

_____

_____

_____

_____

_____

_____

_____

Answer Key

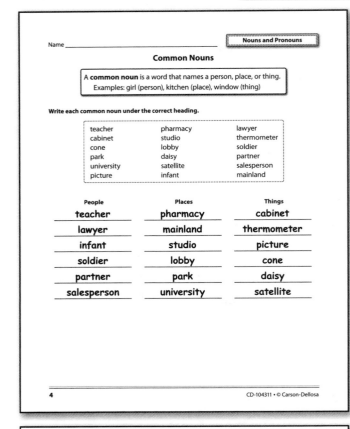

Name _____

Nouns and Pronouns

Common Nouns

> A **common noun** is a word that names a person, place, or thing.
> Examples: girl (person), kitchen (place), window (thing)

Write each common noun under the correct heading.

teacher	pharmacy	lawyer
cabinet	studio	thermometer
cone	lobby	soldier
park	daisy	partner
university	satellite	salesperson
picture	infant	mainland

People	Places	Things
teacher	pharmacy	cabinet
lawyer	mainland	thermometer
infant	studio	picture
soldier	lobby	cone
partner	park	daisy
salesperson	university	satellite

4 CD-104311 • © Carson-Dellosa

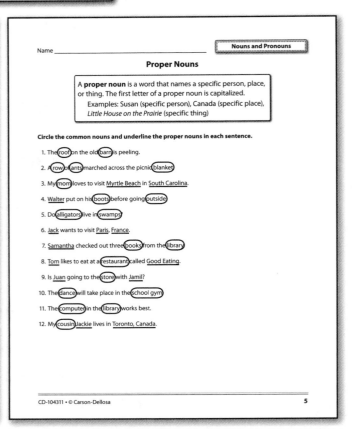

Name _____

Nouns and Pronouns

Proper Nouns

> A **proper noun** is a word that names a specific person, place, or thing. The first letter of a proper noun is capitalized.
> Examples: Susan (specific person), Canada (specific place), *Little House on the Prairie* (specific thing)

Circle the common nouns and underline the proper nouns in each sentence.

1. The (roof) on the old (barn) is peeling.
2. A (row) of (ants) marched across the picnic (blanket).
3. My (mom) loves to visit <u>Myrtle Beach</u> in <u>South Carolina</u>.
4. <u>Walter</u> put on his (boots) before going (outside).
5. Do (alligators) live in (swamps)?
6. <u>Jack</u> wants to visit <u>Paris</u>, <u>France</u>.
7. <u>Samantha</u> checked out three (books) from the (library).
8. <u>Tom</u> likes to eat at a (restaurant) called <u>Good Eating</u>.
9. Is <u>Juan</u> going to the (store) with <u>Jamil</u>?
10. The (dance) will take place in the (school gym).
11. The (computer) in the (library) works best.
12. My (cousin) <u>Jackie</u> lives in <u>Toronto, Canada</u>.

CD-104311 • © Carson-Dellosa 5

Name _____

Nouns and Pronouns

Concrete and Abstract Nouns

> A **concrete noun** identifies something that can be seen, heard, smelled, touched, or tasted.
> Examples: popcorn, theater, music
>
> An **abstract noun** is a word that names an idea or quality that cannot be physically interacted with.
> Examples: memory, kindness, love

Write C for each concrete noun and A for each abstract noun.

1. joy _____A_____
2. bravery _____A_____
3. hair _____C_____
4. imagination _____A_____
5. peach _____C_____
6. freedom _____A_____
7. shout _____C_____
8. guitar _____C_____

Decide if the noun *pride* is a concrete noun or an abstract noun. Explain your decision.

Answers will vary.

6 CD-104311 • © Carson-Dellosa

Name _____

Nouns and Pronouns

Singular and Plural Nouns

> A **singular noun** names one person, place, thing, or idea.
> A **plural noun** names more than one person, place, thing, or idea.
> Add *s* to most singular nouns to make them plural.
> Example: book → books
>
> If a singular noun ends with *sh*, *ch*, *x*, *s*, or *z*, add *es* to make it plural.
> Example: beach → beaches
>
> If a singular noun ends with a consonant followed by *y*, change the *y* to *i* and add *es* to make the word plural.
> Example: baby → babies
>
> If the singular noun ends with a vowel followed by *y*, just add *s* to make the plural.
> Example: boy → boys

Write the plural form of each singular noun.

1. crash	crashes	9. glimpse	glimpses
2. comic	comics	10. responsibility	responsibilities
3. lady	ladies	11. business	businesses
4. dentist	dentists	12. tax	taxes
5. suggestion	suggestions	13. poster	posters
6. decision	decisions	14. dress	dresses
7. address	addresses	15. tortilla	tortillas
8. branch	branches	16. melody	melodies

CD-104311 • © Carson-Dellosa 7

---

104 CD-104311 • © Carson-Dellosa

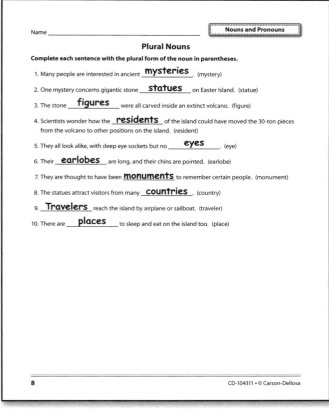

Name _____   **Nouns and Pronouns**

Plural Nouns

Complete each sentence with the plural form of the noun in parentheses.

1. Many people are interested in ancient **mysteries**. (mystery)

2. One mystery concerns gigantic stone **statues** on Easter Island. (statue)

3. The stone **figures** were all carved inside an extinct volcano. (figure)

4. Scientists wonder how the **residents** of the island could have moved the 30-ton pieces from the volcano to other positions on the island. (resident)

5. They all look alike, with deep eye sockets but no **eyes**. (eye)

6. Their **earlobes** are long, and their chins are pointed. (earlobe)

7. They are thought to have been **monuments** to remember certain people. (monument)

8. The statues attract visitors from many **countries**. (country)

9. **Travelers** reach the island by airplane or sailboat. (traveler)

10. There are **places** to sleep and eat on the island too. (place)

8   CD-104311 • © Carson-Dellosa

Name _____   **Nouns and Pronouns**

Plural Nouns

Write the plural form of each singular noun.

1. stereo	**stereos**	15. sandwich	**sandwiches**
2. juice	**juices**	16. wash	**washes**
3. watch	**watches**	17. fox	**foxes**
4. wife	**wives**	18. calf	**calves**
5. wolf	**wolves**	19. radio	**radios**
6. shelf	**shelves**	20. cry	**cries**
7. puppy	**puppies**	21. city	**cities**
8. baby	**babies**	22. jelly	**jellies**
9. hobby	**hobbies**	23. strawberry	**strawberries**
10. glass	**glasses**	24. chimney	**chimneys**
11. boy	**boys**	25. toy	**toys**
12. bay	**bays**	26. turkey	**turkeys**
13. domino	**dominoes**	27. potato	**potatoes**
14. hero	**heroes**	28. video	**videos**

CD-104311 • © Carson-Dellosa   9

Name _____   **Nouns and Pronouns**

Possessive Nouns

A **possessive noun** shows ownership or belonging.

If a noun is singular or if it is plural but does not end with an *s*, add an apostrophe plus an *s* ('s) to the end to make it possessive.
    Examples: dog's food, teacher's pen, men's belts

If a noun is plural and ends with an *s*, add an apostrophe (') to the end.
    Examples: cats' collars, dancers' shoes

Change each phrase into a phrase that uses a possessive noun.

Example: the car belonging to the family → the family's car

1. the toys belonging to the brothers
   brothers' toys

2. the brush belonging to Iris
   Iris's brush

3. the doll belonging to the twins
   twins' doll

4. the bike belonging to his sister
   his sister's bike

Circle each possessive noun. Write *S* if it is singular possessive or *P* if it is plural possessive.

S 5. The (dog's) new leather collar is lost.

P 6. The (snails') aquarium needed cleaning.

S 7. The art (project's) colors were faded by the sun.

P 8. The copier is in the (teachers') workroom.

10   CD-104311 • © Carson-Dellosa

Name _____   **Nouns and Pronouns**

Subject and Object Pronouns

A **subject pronoun** is a pronoun that replaces a noun as the subject of a sentence.

He, she, it, we, and *they* are examples of subject pronouns that can replace nouns or phrases with nouns in the subject of a sentence.
    Example: *Robert Browning* was a poet. → *He* was a poet.

You and *I* are examples of subject pronouns that do not need a reference to the noun or phrase that they are replacing.
    Example: *You* and *I* enjoy his poetry.

An **object pronoun** is a pronoun that replaces a noun in the predicate of a sentence.

Him, her, it, us, and *them* are examples of object pronouns that can replace a noun or phrase with nouns in the predicate of a sentence.
    Example: Robert Browning married *Elizabeth Barrett* in 1846. → Robert Browning married *her* in 1846.

You and *me* are examples of object pronouns that do not need a reference to the noun or phrase that they are replacing.
    Example: Mother reads the Brownings' poetry to *you* and *me*.

Rewrite each sentence using a subject or object pronoun for each underlined word or phrase.

1. Robert was interested in writing about <u>people who lived in the past</u>.
   Robert was interested in writing about them.

2. <u>Elizabeth Barrett Browning</u> was a poet during the Victorian period in England.
   She was a poet during the Victorian period in England.

3. <u>Robert</u> admired her poetry, and <u>he</u> wrote to Elizabeth.
   He admired her poetry, and he wrote to Elizabeth.

4. <u>Robert and Elizabeth</u> were married in 1846.
   They were married in 1846.

CD-104311 • © Carson-Dellosa   11

Name _____ Nouns and Pronouns

Possessive Pronouns

> A **possessive pronoun** is a pronoun that takes the place of a possessive noun. A possessive pronoun does not have an apostrophe.
> Example: *Erin's* brush is on the table. → *Her* brush is on the table.
> Possessive pronouns: my, your, his, her, its, our, their, mine, yours, his, hers, ours, theirs

Circle each possessive pronoun. Draw an arrow to the noun that it modifies.

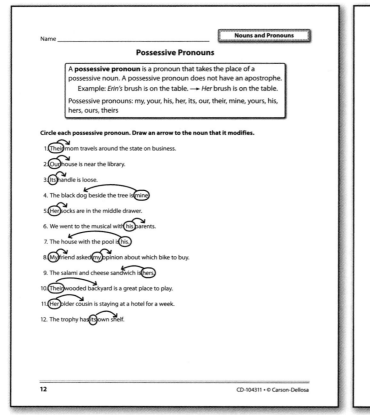

1. Their mom travels around the state on business.
2. Our house is near the library.
3. Its handle is loose.
4. The black dog beside the tree is mine.
5. Her socks are in the middle drawer.
6. We went to the musical with his parents.
7. The house with the pool is his.
8. My friend asked my opinion about which bike to buy.
9. The salami and cheese sandwich is hers.
10. Their wooded backyard is a great place to play.
11. Her older cousin is staying at a hotel for a week.
12. The trophy has its own shelf.

12   CD-104311 • © Carson-Dellosa

Name _____ Nouns and Pronouns

Reflexive Pronouns

> A **reflexive pronoun** is a pronoun that reflects the action of the verb back to the subject.
> Singular reflexive pronouns: myself, yourself, itself, herself, himself
> Example: Leonardo da Vinci painted with a style that made the painting *itself* look misty.
> Plural reflexive pronouns: ourselves, yourselves, themselves
> Example: You all can see the painting's soft and muted colors for *yourselves*.

Write the reflexive pronoun in each sentence on the line.

1. The woman in Leonardo da Vinci's painting, the *Mona Lisa*, seems to be smiling to herself.

 herself

2. For centuries, people have asked themselves why this is so. **themselves**

3. I have wondered myself about her mysterious smile. **myself**

4. Leonardo da Vinci kept that secret to himself. **himself**

5. If you want to see the *Mona Lisa* for yourself, go to the Louvre Museum in Paris, France.

 yourself

Complete each sentence with the correct pronoun in parentheses.

6. Leonardo developed a new painting technique all by **himself**. (itself, himself)

7. The wall **itself** was Leonardo's canvas. (himself, itself)

8. I have tried the technique **myself** and found it challenging. (myself, ourselves)

CD-104311 • © Carson-Dellosa   13

Name _____ Nouns and Pronouns

Indefinite Pronouns

> An **indefinite pronoun** is a pronoun that refers to a noun in a general way.
> Examples: all, another, any, anybody, anyone, anything, both, each, either, everybody, everyone, everything, few, little, many, much, neither, nobody, none, no one, nothing, one, other, others, several, some, somebody, someone, something

Circle the indefinite pronouns in each sentence.

1. Many will come to the museum this summer.
2. A hummingbird came to the feeder this morning, and another came last night.
3. Someone got the crowd cheering excitedly.
4. Only a few registered, but several arrived on the day of the race.
5. I think somebody should clean up the marbles and game pieces.
6. Walter and Mason are here with a mower. Either can mow the yard.
7. If anybody gets home before me, they can put dinner in the oven.
8. Fruits and vegetables are delicious. Each is good for a healthy, growing body.
9. Jessie really wanted to eat both types of cheese.
10. Some have blue tags, and others have red tags.
11. Nothing can be done about the misplaced invitation.
12. All leaves will fall from the trees at the end of summer.
13. Anyone can go to the amusement park.
14. Several swam downstream into the lake.

14   CD-104311 • © Carson-Dellosa

Name _____ Nouns and Pronouns

Interrogative and Demonstrative Pronouns

> An **interrogative pronoun** is a pronoun that introduces a question.
> Interrogative pronouns: who, whom, whose, which, what
> Examples: *Who* is he? *Whom* do you see? *Whose* is this? *Which* of you can help me? *What* is the answer?
> A **demonstrative pronoun** identifies and specifies a noun or pronoun.
> Demonstrative pronouns: this, that, these, and those
> Examples: *This* is nice. *That* is nicer. *These* are fine. *Those* are finer.

Complete each sentence with the correct pronoun in parentheses.

1. **This** is a fact. (This, These)
2. **Those** are little pictures. (That, Those)
3. **What** is the importance of grammar? (What, Which)
4. **These** are not my shoes. (This, These)
5. **That** is an interesting idea. (Those, That)
6. **What** were some of the things you did on vacation? (Whom, What)
7. **Whom** do you know? (That, Whom)
8. **What** were some of the earliest paintings found in Mexico? (Who, What)
9. **Those** are your pancakes. (Those, Whose)
10. **Which** celebration do you like best? (Which, That)

CD-104311 • © Carson-Dellosa   15

Name _____   **Verbs**

Action Verbs

> An **action verb** is a word that expresses action.
> Examples: The audience *applauds* enthusiastically.
> Maria *runs* fast.

Underline the action verb in each sentence.

1. Julie camps in the mountains every summer.

2. Celia finishes her math assignment.

3. She scours the newspaper for the best sales.

4. Mario reviews his answers for each test question.

5. The cow quietly chews the grass.

6. Cynthia picks tomatoes from her garden all summer.

7. Please change the flat tire for me.

8. The sign dangles in the window.

9. The baby squeals with happiness.

10. Mr. Andrews spots the monkey in the tree.

11. Are you watching the football game tonight?

12. My cat drinks water from the faucet outside.

13. Kayla hangs the laundry outside to dry.

14. Lincoln rides his bike for exercise.

16   CD-104311 • © Carson-Dellosa

Name _____   **Verbs**

Linking Verbs

> A **linking verb** is a verb that does not show action. It links or joins the subject of a sentence to information about the subject.
>
> Forms of the verb *be* are the most common linking verbs. There are eight forms of the verb *be*: am, are, is, was, were, (will) be, (am, are, was, were) being, (have, has, had) been.
>   Example: The soup *is* wonderful.
>
> Other linking verbs include forms of these verbs: appear, become, feel, grow, look, remain, seem, smell, sound, taste.
>   Example: The soup *tastes* wonderful.

Underline the linking verb in each sentence.

1. The knitted mittens are very warm.

2. The food on the table appears fresh.

3. The neighbor's dog was sprayed by a skunk.

4. The garbage can by the door is full.

5. That frozen dessert tastes fruity.

6. The letters my mother sent grow more special to me every year.

7. Haley, April's big sister, is our junior counselor.

8. Amber, my younger cousin, will be in first grade next year.

9. The moon was like a huge orange ball hovering in the sky.

10. The music grew increasingly louder.

11. Ms. Tolio, my mom's friend, is a pediatric surgeon.

12. Mom's new scissors are sharp enough to cut cardboard.

13. Dr. Grogan, my orthodontist, is nice.

14. Last night, the moon was low in the sky.

CD-104311 • © Carson-Dellosa   17

Name _____   **Verbs**

Helping Verbs and Verb Phrases

> **Helping verbs** are verbs that help main verbs tell when the action takes place.
>
> There are 23 helping verbs:
>
> be, am, are, is, was, were, being, been   may, must, might
> do, does, did   will, can, shall
> have, has, had   could, would, should
>
> Up to three helping verbs can precede the main verb. The main verb together with its helping verb or verbs makes a verb phrase.
>   Example: I *will talk* to my friend.
>   I *will have talked* to my friend.
>   I *will have been talking* to my friend.

Circle the helping verbs in each sentence. Underline the verb phrases.

1. Sari did jump on the trampoline.

2. The water is pouring into the basement.

3. The rabbit had scurried into the hole.

4. We are going to the amusement park.

5. I am excited to be here.

6. The lights can be dimmed with this switch.

7. Max was taking his turn.

8. The puppy must have tried to jump onto the bed.

9. That jam would make a good sandwich.

10. The bird had flown into the bushes.

11. We should pull the weeds out of the garden.

12. Emma may have been going to the zoo.

18   CD-104311 • © Carson-Dellosa

Name _____   **Verbs**

Present, Past, and Future Tense Action Verbs

> **Verb tenses** tell when the action of a verb happens.
>
> A **present tense action verb** tells about an action that is happening now.
>   Example: Companies *develop* new medicines from plants.
>
> A **past tense action verb** tells about an action that has already happened.
>   Example: People *discovered* that many plants could cure illnesses.
>
> A **future tense action verb** tells about an action that will happen in the future.
>   Example: People *will continue* to search for new medicines.

Circle the action verb in each sentence. Write the tense (present, past, or future) of the action verb on the line.

1. The barber cuts Owen's hair. **present**

2. I will study hard for the test tomorrow. **future**

3. Tim carried his own luggage to the security gate. **past**

4. Barney suddenly leaped into the air for no good reason. **past**

5. She talks with her mom about dinner. **present**

6. Natasha will turn 12 next week. **future**

7. Aaron planted tomatoes, peppers, and cucumbers in his garden. **past**

8. Melody will laugh when she reads my birthday card. **future**

9. Ms. McGuire listens to the radio in the morning. **present**

CD-104311 • © Carson-Dellosa   19

Answer Key

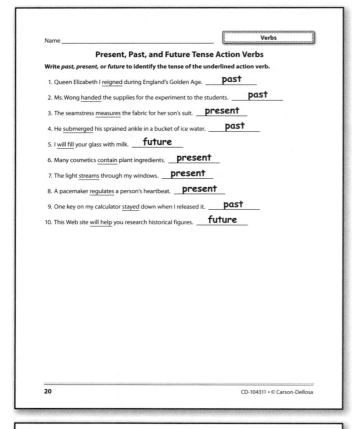

Name _____   Verbs

Present, Past, and Future Tense Action Verbs

Write past, present, or future to identify the tense of the underlined action verb.

1. Queen Elizabeth I <u>reigned</u> during England's Golden Age. __past__
2. Ms. Wong <u>handed</u> the supplies for the experiment to the students. __past__
3. The seamstress <u>measures</u> the fabric for her son's suit. __present__
4. He <u>submerged</u> his sprained ankle in a bucket of ice water. __past__
5. I will <u>fill</u> your glass with milk. __future__
6. Many cosmetics <u>contain</u> plant ingredients. __present__
7. The light <u>streams</u> through my windows. __present__
8. A pacemaker <u>regulates</u> a person's heartbeat. __present__
9. One key on my calculator <u>stayed</u> down when I released it. __past__
10. This Web site will <u>help</u> you research historical figures. __future__

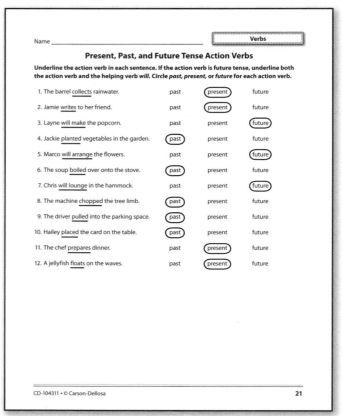

Name _____   Verbs

Present, Past, and Future Tense Action Verbs

Underline the action verb in each sentence. If the action verb is future tense, underline both the action verb and the helping verb *will*. Circle *past, present,* or *future* for each action verb.

1. The barrel <u>collects</u> rainwater.   past   (present)   future
2. Jamie <u>writes</u> to her friend.   past   (present)   future
3. Layne will <u>make</u> the popcorn.   past   present   (future)
4. Jackie <u>planted</u> vegetables in the garden.   (past)   present   future
5. Marco will <u>arrange</u> the flowers.   past   present   (future)
6. The soup <u>boiled</u> over onto the stove.   (past)   present   future
7. Chris will <u>lounge</u> in the hammock.   past   present   (future)
8. The machine <u>chopped</u> the tree limb.   (past)   present   future
9. The driver <u>pulled</u> into the parking space. (past)   present   future
10. Hailey <u>placed</u> the card on the table.   (past)   present   future
11. The chef <u>prepares</u> dinner.   past   (present)   future
12. A jellyfish <u>floats</u> on the waves.   past   (present)   future

Name _____   Verbs

Past Tense Verbs

> Remember, the past tense is used to show action that has already happened.
>
> Usually, *ed* or *d* is added to a verb to form the past tense.
>   Examples: walk → walked
>   wave → waved
> If a verb ends with a consonant + *y*, change *y* to *i* and add *ed*.
>   Example: carry → carried
> If a verb has a short vowel with one consonant, double the consonant and add *ed*.
>   Examples: hop → hopped
>   stop → stopped

Write the past tense of each verb.

1. rustle __rustled__   6. end   __ended__
2. bat   __batted__   7. cry   __cried__
3. lunge   __lunged__   8. sip   __sipped__
4. agree   __agreed__   9. snap   __snapped__
5. ship   __shipped__   10. create __created__

Complete each sentence with the past tense of the verb in parentheses.

11. Julio __copied__ his work onto clean paper. (copy)
12. The kitten __pounced__ on the ladybug. (pounce)
13. Quincy __tried__ spinach for the first time. (try)
14. Paulo __hurried__ to his piano lesson. (hurry)
15. Annabelle __played__ a game with her cousin. (play)
16. Brett __shopped__ for comfortable shoes. (shop)

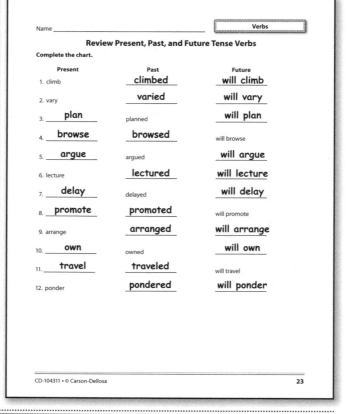

Name _____   Verbs

Review Present, Past, and Future Tense Verbs

Complete the chart.

Present	Past	Future
1. climb	climbed	will climb
2. vary	varied	will vary
3. plan	planned	will plan
4. browse	browsed	will browse
5. argue	argued	will argue
6. lecture	lectured	will lecture
7. delay	delayed	will delay
8. promote	promoted	will promote
9. arrange	arranged	will arrange
10. own	owned	will own
11. travel	traveled	will travel
12. ponder	pondered	will ponder

Page 24 — Infinitives

Name _____   **Verbs**

Infinitives

A verb has four principal parts: present (infinitive), present participle, past, and past participle.

An **infinitive** is the *to* form of a verb. It is composed of the word *to* and what is called the base form, or most basic form, of a verb.

Examples: to be
            to sleep
            to eat

Circle the infinitives in each sentence.

1. We need (to water) the plants.
2. Lee's goal was (to be) outstanding.
3. It takes strength (to open) the jar.
4. You will need (to remove) the plastic liner.
5. A ticket is needed (to enter) the movie theater.
6. My friend brought a game for us (to play).
7. We want (to enjoy) the movie without a lot of extra noise.
8. Many people like (to drink) from the drinking fountain.
9. Abby and Pearl want (to show) the class how to make pancakes.
10. We will be ready (to leave) when all of the toys are picked up.
11. The buds on the yellow flowers are beginning (to open).
12. Dad is driving across town (to buy) more wood.

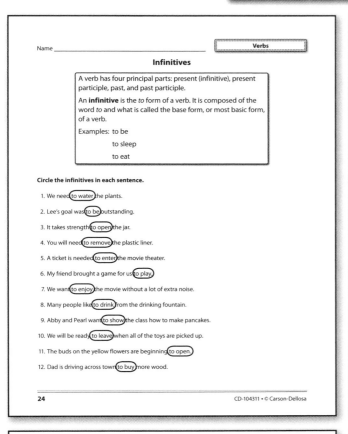

24   CD-104311 • © Carson-Dellosa

Page 25 — Present and Past Participles

Name _____   **Verbs**

Present and Past Participles

The **present participle** is formed by adding *ing* to the base form of a verb.
   Example: Base form: rock → Present participle: rocking

The **past participle** is usually formed by adding *ed* or *d* to the base form of a verb and is the same as the past tense form of the verb.
   Example: Base form: rock → Past participle: rocked

Some irregular verbs have past participles that are not formed by adding *ed* or *d* and may not be the same as the past tense form of the verb.
   Example: Base form: see → Past participle: seen

Complete the chart.

Present	Present Participle	Past	Past Participle
1. work	working	worked	worked
2. walk	walking	walked	walked
3. view	viewing	viewed	viewed
4. call	calling	called	called
5. plant	planting	planted	planted
6. leap	leaping	leaped	leaped

Draw a line to the correct past participle of each irregular verb.

7. break — broken
8. tear — torn
9. bring — brought
10. choose — chosen
11. go — gone
12. begin — begun

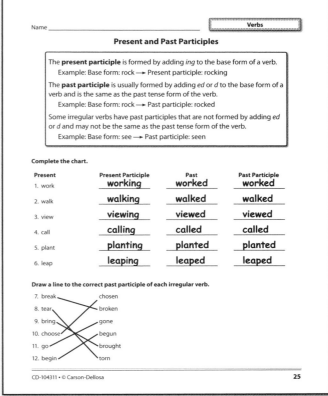

CD-104311 • © Carson-Dellosa   25

Page 26 — Past Participle of Irregular Verbs

Name _____   **Verbs**

Past Participle of Irregular Verbs

The past participle of an irregular verb can be the same as or different from the past tense form of the verb. Past participles of irregular verbs often end with *t*, *en*, or *n*.

Examples:

Present	Past	Past Participle
ring	rang	rung
wear	wore	worn
blow	blew	blown

Complete each sentence with the correct past participle in the parentheses.

1. The mother blue jay has __sat__ on her eggs for many days. (sitted, sat)
2. Mr. Wu has __chosen__ to take the subway to work this morning. (chose, chosen)
3. The towering old pine had __fallen__ during the snowstorm. (fell, fallen)
4. Rick has __spoken__ on the phone for two hours. (spoked, spoken)
5. The girls had __swung__ on the tire swing before us. (swinged, swung)
6. Ralph and Perry have __swum__ in Lake Michigan before. (swimmed, swum)
7. The goat at the zoo had __eaten__ the food on the ground. (ate, eaten)
8. Tyrone had __set__ his camera on the picnic table. (setted, set)
9. The mother of the groom has __made__ the wedding cake. (maked, made)
10. The fishermen had __risen__ before the sun came up. (arosed, risen)
11. Cyndi has __caught__ several butterflies in her net. (catched, caught)
12. That hornet had __stung__ Sasha's hand. (stinged, stung)
13. Xena and Sean __slid__ down the snowy hill on their sled. (slided, slid)
14. The vase has __broken__ into pieces on the floor. (broke, broken)

26   CD-104311 • © Carson-Dellosa

Page 27 — Past Participle of Irregular Verbs

Name _____   **Verbs**

Past Participle of Irregular Verbs

Fill in the chart with the correct forms of the irregular verbs. Refer to a dictionary, if needed.

Present	Past	Past Participle
1. draw	drew	drawn
2. swim	swam	swum
3. teach	taught	taught

Complete each sentence with the past tense of the irregular verb in parentheses.

4. Two men __stood__ at the foot of the Pennine Alps. (stand)
5. Heavy snow __fell__, and the storm raged around them. (fall)
6. They __saw__ only snow, ice, and the mountain. (see)

Complete each sentence with the past participle of the irregular verb in parentheses.

7. They have __thought__ of climbing the mountain for months. (think)
8. The men have __known__ it would be difficult to climb at this time of year. (know)
9. They have __chosen__ to wait to climb until the weather is clear. (choose)

CD-104311 • © Carson-Dellosa   27

Page 28

Name _____   Verbs

Present Perfect, Past Perfect, and Future Perfect Verbs

The **present perfect tense** of a verb indicates action that has been completed or that extends into the present. It is formed by adding the word *have* or *has* before the past participle.
Examples: I *have gone* to that shop before.
Julio *has gone* to that shop before.

The **past perfect tense** of a verb indicates action that was completed before something else happened. It is formed by adding the word *had* before the past participle.
Examples: I *had gone* by the time he arrived.
Julio *had gone* by the time he arrived.

The **future perfect tense** of a verb indicates action that will have been completed in the future before something else happens. It is formed by adding the words *will have* before the past participle.
Examples: I *will have gone* by the time he arrives.
Julio *will have gone* by the time he arrives.

Rewrite each sentence using the perfect tense for each verb in parentheses.

1. Since Tommy _____ his homework, he was free the rest of the evening. (do, past perfect)
Since Tommy had done his homework, he was free the rest of the evening.

2. I _____ a marathon two months before I run the Boston Marathon. (run, future perfect)
I will have run a full marathon two months before I run the Boston Marathon.

3. Mom _____ countless numbers of doors for me since I broke my leg. (open, present perfect)
Mom has opened countless numbers of doors for me since I broke my leg.

4. Reenie said they _____ to Connecticut five times after they take their trip. (go, future perfect)
Reenie said they will have gone to Connecticut five times after they take their trip.

28 — CD-104311 • © Carson-Dellosa

Page 29

Name _____   Verbs

Present Perfect Tense

Write the present perfect tense of the verb in parentheses in each sentence.

1. Lightning **has started** a fire in Yellowstone National Park. (start)
2. The old spruce and fir trees **have burned** quickly. (burn)
3. Flaming twigs **have ignited** dry leaves on the forest floor. (ignite)
4. The winds **have picked** up, and the fire has intensified. (pick)
5. The wildfire **has moved** up the valley rapidly. (move)
6. The governor **has requested** that many counties evacuate. (request)
7. Organizations **have urged** people to gather items for families in need. (urge)
8. The teachers, staff, and students at my school **have donated** many items to help people. (donate)
9. Many people **have helped** the families during this difficult time. (help)
10. I hope that the firefighters **have extinguished** the fire. (extinguish)

CD-104311 • © Carson-Dellosa — 29

Page 30

Name _____   Verbs

Verb Tense Review

Circle the verb in each sentence below. Then, identify the tense of each verb. Use the abbreviations below.

SPRE—simple present   SF—simple future
PASTP—past perfect   SPAST—simple past
PREP—present perfect   FP—future perfect

PASTP 1. Kenzie (had seen) the other team arrive before the game.
SF 2. (will support) Andrew for our student government representative.
SPRE 3. The wind (blows) rapidly this time of year.
SF 4. (Can) I please (study) with you next time?
FP 5. Marie (will have gone) home by then!
SPAST 6. Alexander Graham Bell (invented) the telephone in 1876.
PASTP 7. Lexie (had talked) to Mr. Brown about her math test after school.
PASTP 8. The team (had hoped) for more wins this year.
PREP 9. The students (have studied) for many hours for the test.
PREP 10. Renee (has talked) with the guidance counselor.
SF 11. Mom (will follow) us to the restaurant.
PREP 12. David (has decided) to buy the yellow hat.

30 — CD-104311 • © Carson-Dellosa

Page 31

Name _____   Verbs

Present Progressive and Past Progressive Tenses

The **present progressive tense** of a verb tells about ongoing action happening in the present.
Use forms of *be* (*am, is,* and *are*) with the present participle to form the present progressive tense.
Example: The clouds *are growing* in intensity.

The **past progressive tense** of a verb tells about an ongoing action that happened in the past and is now completed.
Use past tense forms of *be* (*was* and *were*) with the present participle to form the past progressive tense.
Example: The winds *were beginning* to change direction.

Write each sentence twice. Write the first with the present progressive tense of the verb in parentheses. Write the second with the past progressive tense of the verb in parentheses.

The scientist _____ the discovery of fossils in the ground. (explain)
1. **is explaining**
2. **was explaining**

The ballerinas _____ into the air. (leap)
3. **are leaping**
4. **were leaping**

Dan _____ for our teacher today. (substitute)
5. **is substituting**
6. **was substituting**

CD-104311 • © Carson-Dellosa — 31

---

110   CD-104311 • © Carson-Dellosa

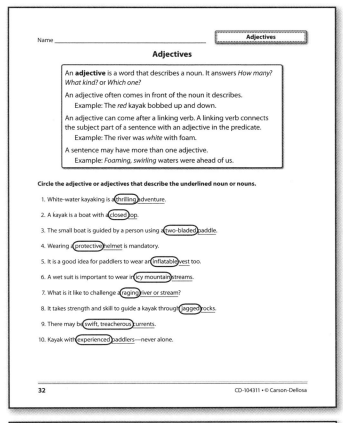

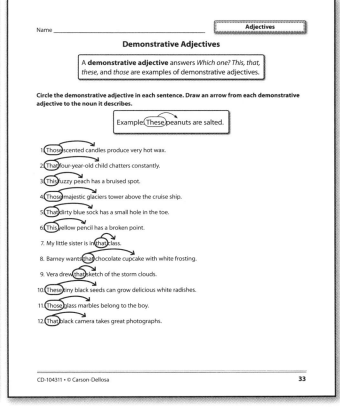

Name _____

Adjectives

Adjectives

An **adjective** is a word that describes a noun. It answers *How many? What kind?* or *Which one?*

An adjective often comes in front of the noun it describes.
Example: The *red* kayak bobbed up and down.

An adjective can come after a linking verb. A linking verb connects the subject part of a sentence with an adjective in the predicate.
Example: The river was *white* with foam.

A sentence may have more than one adjective.
Example: *Foaming, swirling* waters were ahead of us.

Circle the adjective or adjectives that describe the underlined noun or nouns.

1. White-water kayaking is a thrilling adventure.
2. A kayak is a boat with a closed top.
3. The small boat is guided by a person using a two-bladed paddle.
4. Wearing a protective helmet is mandatory.
5. It is a good idea for paddlers to wear an inflatable vest too.
6. A wet suit is important to wear in icy mountain streams.
7. What is it like to challenge a raging river or stream?
8. It takes strength and skill to guide a kayak through jagged rocks.
9. There may be swift, treacherous currents.
10. Kayak with experienced paddlers—never alone.

32   CD-104311 • © Carson-Dellosa

Name _____

Adjectives

Demonstrative Adjectives

A **demonstrative adjective** answers *Which one? This, that, these,* and *those* are examples of demonstrative adjectives.

Circle the demonstrative adjective in each sentence. Draw an arrow from each demonstrative adjective to the noun it describes.

Example: These peanuts are salted.

1. Those scented candles produce very hot wax.
2. That four-year-old child chatters constantly.
3. This fuzzy peach has a bruised spot.
4. Those majestic glaciers tower above the cruise ship.
5. That dirty blue sock has a small hole in the toe.
6. This yellow pencil has a broken point.
7. My little sister is in that class.
8. Barney wants that chocolate cupcake with white frosting.
9. Vera drew that sketch of the storm clouds.
10. These tiny black seeds can grow delicious white radishes.
11. Those glass marbles belong to the boy.
12. That black camera takes great photographs.

CD-104311 • © Carson-Dellosa   33

Name _____

Adjectives

Limiting and Descriptive Adjectives

A **descriptive adjective** adds details to a noun and answers *What kind?*
Examples: *shabby* couch, *honest* friend

A **limiting adjective** tells a quantity or number and answers *How many?*
Examples: *one* sign, a *few* apples

Underline each descriptive adjective and circle each limiting adjective.

1. Our dog had four puppies.
2. I love to sit in front of a crackling fire.
3. Let's toast delicious marshmallows!
4. I need five notebooks for school.
5. Did you see the spotted leopard?
6. May I have two more cookies?
7. I would like a glass of cold milk.
8. Please hand me a few grapes.

34   CD-104311 • © Carson-Dellosa

Name _____

Adjectives

Comparative and Superlative Adjectives

Some adjectives compare nouns.

A **comparative adjective** compares two nouns. Usually, a comparative adjective is formed by adding *er* to an adjective.
Example: tall → taller

A **superlative adjective** compares more than two nouns. Usually, a superlative adjective is formed by adding *est* to an adjective.
Example: short → shortest

If an adjective ends with *e*, drop the *e* and add *er* or *est*.
Example: rare → rarest

If an adjective ends in a consonant + *y*, change *y* to *i* and add *er* or *est*.
Example: funny → funnier

If an adjective has a short vowel and ends with one consonant, double the consonant and add *er* or *est*.
Example: mad → madder

If an adjective has two or more syllables, use *more, most, less,* or *least* before it.
Example: wonderful → most wonderful

Write the comparative and superlative forms of each adjective.

	Comparative	Superlative
1. happy	happier	happiest
2. wise	wiser	wisest
3. fast	faster	fastest
4. great	greater	greatest
5. delicious	more delicious	most delicious
6. interesting	more interesting	most interesting
7. vibrant	more vibrant	most vibrant
8. majestic	more majestic	most majestic

CD-104311 • © Carson-Dellosa   35

Name _____

Comparative and Superlative Adjectives

Circle the correct form of the adjective in each sentence.

1. The (**nearest**, more near) restaurant is four miles away.

2. This hot chocolate is (**hotter**, most hot) than I like it.

3. My friend Pedro is the (most nice, **nicest**) person I know.

4. That movie was (**funnier**, funniest) than the one we watched last week.

5. This book is (intense, **less intense**) than its sequel.

6. This assignment is (**harder**, more hard) than yesterday's was.

7. The (**best**, more best) meals are those roasted above an open fire.

8. I was the (**least excited**, excited) of all my friends about going to the water park.

9. That batch of applesauce is (**sweeter**, more sweeter) than this batch.

10. Your head is (**most protected**, more protect) with a bike helmet.

CD-104311 • © Carson-Dellosa

Name _____

Predicate Adjectives

A **predicate adjective** modifies or describes a noun or pronoun like other adjectives, but it must follow a linking verb in a sentence.
Examples: This cake is *good*. (*good* describes *cake*)
Her hair looks *shiny*. (*shiny* describes *hair*)

Underline the predicate adjective in each sentence. Draw an arrow to the noun or pronoun that it modifies.

1. The cookies smell delicious.

2. You look happy.

3. Matt is sick today.

4. The bananas are ripe.

5. His party was fun!

6. The alarm sounds loud.

7. The air became cool after the storm.

8. Lena's bag is heavy!

CD-104311 • © Carson-Dellosa

Name _____

Articles

A, *an*, and *the* are special adjectives called **articles**.
Use *a* to describe any singular noun that begins with a consonant sound.
　　Example: a teacher
Use *an* to describe any singular noun that begins with a vowel sound.
　　Example: an analyst
Use *the* with singular or plural nouns to tell about a particular person, place, or thing.
　　Example: the typist

Write *a* or *an* in front of each singular noun. Write *the* in front of each plural noun.

1. **an** employee
2. **a** doctor
3. **a** professional
4. **an** actress
5. **the** monarchs
6. **the** candidates
7. **a** designer
8. **an** official

9. **an** architect
10. **the** rangers
11. **the** troopers
12. **the** musicians
13. **a** forester
14. **an** operator
15. **a** gymnast
16. **the** instructors

CD-104311 • © Carson-Dellosa

Name _____

Articles

Use the articles *a* and *an* correctly with the phrases below.

1. **a** cave explorer
2. **an** impressive cobbler
3. **a** nuclear engineer
4. **an** excited salesperson
5. **an** accomplished writer
6. **a** professional artist
7. **a** radio announcer
8. **a** remarkable ecologist
9. **an** outstanding poet
10. **a** brave astronaut
11. **an** angry bee
12. **a** good friend
13. **a** funny movie
14. **an** incredible game
15. **a** soft blanket

CD-104311 • © Carson-Dellosa

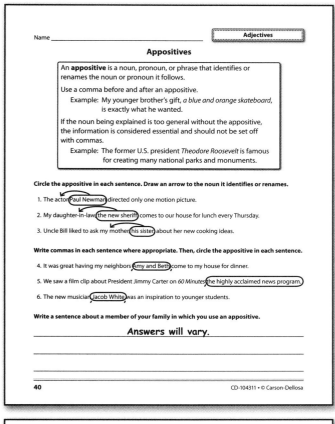

Name _____   **Adjectives**

Appositives

An **appositive** is a noun, pronoun, or phrase that identifies or renames the noun or pronoun it follows.

Use a comma before and after an appositive.
    Example: My younger brother's gift, *a blue and orange skateboard,* is exactly what he wanted.

If the noun being explained is too general without the appositive, the information is considered essential and should not be set off with commas.
    Example: The former U.S. president *Theodore Roosevelt* is famous for creating many national parks and monuments.

Circle the appositive in each sentence. Draw an arrow to the noun it identifies or renames.

1. The actor Paul Newman directed only one motion picture.

2. My daughter-in-law, the new sheriff comes to our house for lunch every Thursday.

3. Uncle Bill liked to ask my mother, his sister about her new cooking ideas.

Write commas in each sentence where appropriate. Then, circle the appositive in each sentence.

4. It was great having my neighbors, Amy and Beth, come to my house for dinner.

5. We saw a film clip about President Jimmy Carter on *60 Minutes,* the highly acclaimed news program.

6. The new musician Jacob White was an inspiration to younger students.

Write a sentence about a member of your family in which you use an appositive.

Answers will vary.

40   CD-104311 • © Carson-Dellosa

Name _____   **Adverbs**

Adverbs

An **adverb** is a word that describes a verb or an adjective. Adverbs answer *Where? When? How often? How?* or *To what extent?*
    Example: Please speak *quietly* in the library.

Complete each sentence with an adverb from the box. Use each word once.

truthfully   never   early   quickly
tomorrow   loudly   quietly   excitedly

1. The witness answered the question **truthfully**.
2. We ran **quickly** to get out of the rain.
3. She arrived at the movie 10 minutes **early**.
4. We spoke **quietly** while the baby was sleeping.
5. Can you come over to my house **tomorrow**?
6. I **never** stay up after 9:00 P.M. on school nights.
7. She cried **loudly** when she broke her arm.
8. Anna **excitedly** opened her birthday present.

CD-104311 • © Carson-Dellosa   41

Name _____   **Adverbs**

Time Adverbs

A time adverb answers *When?* or *How often?*
    Examples: before, continuously, early, eventually, finally, first, frequently, immediately, last night, lately, never, nightly, now, often, once, periodically, rarely, sometimes, soon, then, today, tonight, tomorrow, usually

Complete each sentence with a time adverb. Use an adverb only once.

Answers will vary.

Brett

Brett _____ loses his glasses. They are _____ found in odd places. His glasses are _____ found on the drinking fountain. He even left them on the soccer field _____. Brett's puppy found his glasses _____. After playing with them for a while, the puppy brought the glasses to Brett _____. Brett promised his mom _____ to leave his glasses lying around again.

Sylvia

Sylvia _____ is awake and attentive. However, she is very tired _____. Sylvia did not get much sleep _____. Her baby brother is sick and cried _____. Sylvia _____ drifted off to sleep. Hopefully, she and her brother will both sleep better _____.

42   CD-104311 • © Carson-Dellosa

Name _____   **Adverbs**

Place Adverbs

A place adverb answers *Where?*
    Examples: anywhere, here, down, there, upstairs, underground, everywhere, away

Circle the place adverbs in each sentence. There may be more than one adverb in a sentence.

1. Many crawly things live outside.
2. I like them better there than inside.
3. They seem to be everywhere you look.
4. They are below, above, and beside you.
5. Ants congregate underground.
6. Worms live there too.
7. Mosquitoes seem to be anywhere people are.
8. One buzzed close to my ear the other day.
9. It seems insects are always nearby.
10. Dragonflies like to hover overhead.
11. Caterpillars sometimes crawl inside a tree trunk.
12. I know insects are helpful to nature, but I would not mind if they stayed far from me!

CD-104311 • © Carson-Dellosa   43

Name _____ Adverbs

Manner Adverbs

A **manner adverb** answers *How?* or *In what manner?* Some manner adverbs end in *ly*.

Examples: closely, well, cheerfully, fast, slowly, happily, calmly, bravely, kindly, safely, perfectly, softly, hourly, joyously

Circle the manner adverb in each sentence.

1. The kitten and puppy (playfully) ran from one end of the room to the other.
2. Jolene's foot tapped (nervously).
3. Liza smiled (confidently) as she stood at the free-throw line.
4. The children waited (expectantly) for the movie to begin.
5. The fireworks exploded (brightly) in the night sky.
6. Louis likes to read (aloud) to the kindergartners.
7. Amber and I walked (together) to soccer practice.
8. We were (completely) surprised by the announcement.
9. Owen worked (diligently) to finish his project by Friday.
10. Quincy (carefully) climbed the maple tree to get the kite down.
11. Ian (quickly) rode his bike home in order to meet his curfew.
12. Maddie (intently) watched the ants carry food crumbs into the anthill.
13. Dakota (gently) took the artwork off the wall.
14. Ava's mom (immediately) drenched the fire with water.

44   CD-104311 • © Carson-Dellosa

Name _____ Adverbs

Comparative and Superlative Adverbs

A **comparative adverb** compares two verbs. Usually, a comparative adverb is formed by adding *er* to an adverb.

Example: fast → faster

A **superlative adverb** compares more than two verbs. Usually, a superlative adverb is formed by adding *est* to an adverb.

Example: fast → fastest

Add the word *more* or *less* before adverbs ending in *ly* to compare two verbs.

Example: more carefully

Add the word *most* or *least* before adverbs ending in *ly* when comparing more than two verbs.

Example: most carefully

Some comparative and superlative adverbs have irregular spellings.

Example: far → farther → farthest

Complete the chart with adverbs that compare the actions of verbs.

Adverbs	Comparative	Superlative
1. completely	more completely	most completely
2. fondly	more fondly	most fondly
3. near	nearer	nearest
4. wearily	more wearily	most wearily
5. close	closer	closest
6. brilliantly	more brilliantly	most brilliantly
7. timely	more timely	most timely
8. seriously	more seriously	most seriously

CD-104311 • © Carson-Dellosa   45

Name _____ Adverbs

Comparative and Superlative Adverbs

Complete each sentence with the correct adverb in parentheses.

1. Clark ran his campaign for our student council president **more successfully** than his opponents. (more successfully, most successfully)
2. He made speeches **more often** than his opponents. (most often, more often)
3. Of all the candidates, Clark spoke **most clearly** about his plans for the student government. (more clearly, most clearly)
4. Clark listened **more carefully** than his opponents to the ideas and concerns of his classmates. (more carefully, most carefully)
5. When the teachers announced the winner, the principal clapped the **most loudly**. She was his mom! (more loudly, most loudly)
6. Clark smiled **more broadly** than anyone else in the room. (most broadly, more broadly)

46   CD-104311 • © Carson-Dellosa

Name _____ Punctuation

Capitalization

Capitalize the first word of every sentence.
Example: *We* really should go to the game.

Capitalize the first word in a quotation.
Example: Marnie said, "*You* need help!"

Capitalize all proper nouns.
Example: *Justin* currently lives in *Des Moines, Iowa.*

Capitalize all proper adjectives.
Example: Ruth is a *Canadian* citizen.

Circle the words in each sentence that should be capitalized.

1. "(And) so, my fellow (americans)," said (john f. kennedy), "(ask) not what your country can do for you, ask what you can do for your country."
2. (Sara) and (rachel) were excited to go to the dance at (roosevelt elementary school).
3. (Senators) and representatives together are called the (congress).
4. (If) (tonya) wants to come, my mom can pick her up.
5. (The) (south american) continent is south of the (united states) and (mexico).
6. (Since) we don't have to go to school on (columbus day), I plan to go to (manhattan beach) with (ginger).
7. (I've) always said, "(Do) to your neighbors as you would have them do to you."
8. (People) from all over the world come to the (taj mahal) every year from faraway places such as (japan, canada), and (australia).
9. (If) you think you have time to go to (barton creek grocery), please buy some milk.
10. (Galileo) was an astronomer and physicist from (italy).

CD-104311 • © Carson-Dellosa   47

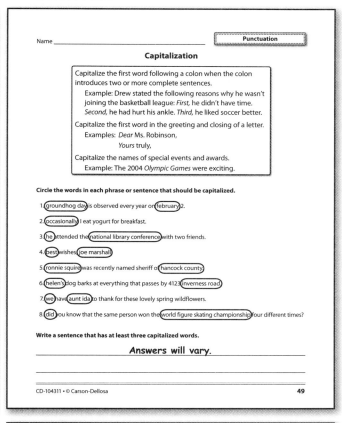

Name _____

Punctuation

Capitalization

> Capitalize a person's title when it comes before a name.
>> Example: *Governor* Jones said that she would veto the new bill.
>
> Capitalize the abbreviations of titles.
>> Example: *Lt.* Elliott was early for her appointment this morning.
>
> Capitalize the first letter in the abbreviations of days and months, and both letters in the abbreviations for states.
>> Examples: *AK, CA, VT, Mon., Wed., Feb., Aug.*
>
> Capitalize the first, last, and all other important words in the titles of books, movies, stories, songs, and poems.
>> Examples: *War* and *Peace*, "*Over* the *Rainbow*"

Circle the words in each sentence that should be capitalized. Refer to the capitalization rules in the previous activity, if necessary.

1. (when) (principal walton) came into the room, everyone stopped talking.
2. I hope (mr. lipson) asks us to read (remember me to harold square) this year.
3. (candice) arrived on (january) 1 and left on (march) 15.
4. (at thirteen,) (sam houston) moved from (virginia) to (tennessee)
5. (the) address on the letter read (georgetown, tx)
6. (jessica) took her dog (mittens) for a long walk around (randolph lake)
7. (my) granddad said, (your) grandma and I are glad you came to visit."
8. (the arizona film festival) featured a film called (the clay bird)
9. (mother's day) is always on a (sunday)
10. (if) you see the movie (the wizard of oz,) let me know what you think.

48   CD-104311 • © Carson-Dellosa

Name _____

Punctuation

Capitalization

> Capitalize the first word following a colon when the colon introduces two or more complete sentences.
>> Example: Drew stated the following reasons why he wasn't joining the basketball league: *First,* he didn't have time. *Second,* he had hurt his ankle. *Third,* he liked soccer better.
>
> Capitalize the first word in the greeting and closing of a letter.
>> Examples: *Dear* Ms. Robinson,
>>
>> *Yours* truly,
>
> Capitalize the names of special events and awards.
>> Example: The 2004 *Olympic Games* were exciting.

Circle the words in each phrase or sentence that should be capitalized.

1. (groundhog day) is observed every year on (february) 2.
2. (occasionally) I eat yogurt for breakfast.
3. (he) attended the (national library conference) with two friends.
4. (best) wishes (joe marshall)
5. (ronnie squire) was recently named sheriff of (hancock county)
6. (helen's) dog barks at everything that passes by 4123 (inverness road)
7. (we) have (aunt ida) to thank for these lovely spring wildflowers.
8. (did) you know that the same person won the (world figure skating championship) four different times?

Write a sentence that has at least three capitalized words.

<u>Answers will vary.</u>

CD-104311 • © Carson-Dellosa   49

Name _____

Punctuation

Commas

> The primary purpose of a **comma** (,) is to prevent misunderstandings. Overuse of commas can make reading more difficult.
>
> Use a comma between words or groups of words in a series.
>> Example: You should take a cap, gloves, and sunglasses to the slopes.
>
> Use a comma before a conjunction that separates independent clauses.
>> Example: Randy wrote the words, and Beth wrote the music.
>
> Use a comma to set off a quotation from the rest of the sentence.
>> Example: Amy said, "Remember your jacket!"
>
> Use a comma to set off words in a direct address.
>> Example: Look out, Mila, it's coming your way.
>
> Use a comma to separate months and days from years (but not months from years).
>> Example: The date was October 12, 1492.
>
> Use a comma to set off an appositive.
>> Example: Michael, Katie's older brother, was just hired by my company.

Write commas in each sentence where they are needed.

1. Gretchen, can you give me a hand?
2. The mural was filled with splashes of blue, green, gold, and red.
3. Mrs. Jackson, my fourth-grade teacher, was always my favorite.
4. You can either come to my house, or I will come to yours.
5. The campers made sure they brought enough food, blankets, and water.
6. "Please show me the way out of here," said Mia.
7. I want to leave, but I am afraid I will miss something.
8. On Saturday, April 18, 2005, I went swimming in Crystal Creek.

50   CD-104311 • © Carson-Dellosa

Name _____

Punctuation

Commas

> Use a comma after the greeting in a friendly letter.
>> Example: Dear Mom,
>
> Use a comma in the closing of a letter.
>> Example: Sincerely,
>
> Use a comma to separate an ordinal number from the rest of the sentence if it is not used as an adjective.
>> Example: First, you must turn on the computer.
>
> Use a comma to separate an introductory word or group of words from the rest of the sentence.
>> Example: Without regret, Jason went to see his old adversary.
>
> Use a comma to separate two or more adjectives modifying the same noun if the word *and* could be inserted between the words without changing the meaning.
>> Example: Jenny is a careful, honest writer.

Write commas in each phrase or sentence where they are needed.

1. Dear Andy, Thank you for coming to play.
2. Fortunately, I have already submitted your application.
3. There are benefits to living in a hot, dry climate.
4. She is supposed to move into her new house on June 14, 2009.
5. Truly yours, Abigail
6. My mother's advice was, "If you can't say something nice, don't say anything at all."
7. I've been thinking a lot about you, and I wish you a speedy recovery.
8. Dr. Randolph, Damon's father, was our troop leader.

CD-104311 • © Carson-Dellosa   51

Page 52 — Hyphens and Dashes

Name _____

Punctuation

Hyphens and Dashes

> Use a hyphen (-) when writing out compound numbers from 21 to 99.
>> Example: sixty-three
>
> Use a hyphen between compound adjectives that come before the noun they modify.
>> Example: French-speaking Canadians
>
> Use a hyphen to separate the syllables of a word that is carried over from one line to the next.
>> Example: We went to the movie and then decided to go to a near-by delicatessen for a snack.
>
> Use an *en* dash (–) to show a range of dates, times, or reference numbers.
>> Example: July–August 2000
>> 1:00 P.M.–3:30 P.M.
>
> Use an *em* dash (—) for emphasis.
>> Example: When I grow up—which seems like it will take forever—I want to play a professional sport.

Write hyphens and dashes in each sentence where they are needed. Write *H* after the sentence if you used a hyphen, and write *D* if you used a dash.

1. The sports–loving fans did not seem to notice the freezing temperature. **H**

2. The book focused on the post–Civil War period. **D**

3. The appointments available are 12:00 P.M.—4:00 P.M. **D**

4. The assignment for tomorrow is to read pages 24–36 carefully. Make certain that you read them because there will be a quiz. **D**

5. Forty-four electric fans are in stock. **H**

6. The Chicago–New York flight lasts less than two hours. **D**

7. We go to great lengths—often far beyond our normal limitations—to win! **D**

8. If I only needed to read chapters 2–4, I would be finished by now. **D**

52   CD-104311 • © Carson-Dellosa

Page 53 — Quotation Marks

Name _____

Punctuation

Quotation Marks

> Use quotation marks (" ") to set off titles of songs, poems, and stories within a collection of other stories.
>> Examples: "The Star-Spangled Banner" (song)
>> "A Good Walk Spoiled" (poem)
>> "The Ugly Duckling" (story within a collection of other stories)
>
> Use quotation marks before and after a direct quote.
>> Example: "There's the bus!" yelled Jon.
>
> If the name of the speaker interrupts the quote, place quotation marks before and after the spoken words. The second part of the quote begins with a lowercase letter if it is a continuation of the first part.
>> Example: "I am really tired," sighed Becca, "because that race was longer than I thought."
>
> Do not use quotation marks with indirect quotes, which tell what someone said but do not use the person's exact words.
>> Example: Mr. Bentley said that he thought we did a good job.

Write quotation marks in each sentence where they are needed.

1. Once out of the storm, Jason shouted, "Hurray! We made it!"

2. "Have you ever been a part of any sports team at your school?" asked Silvia.

3. "After you take out the trash," said my dad, "we can go see a movie."

4. Reid told Angie that "Casey at the Bat" was one of her favorite poems.

5. Many people have suggested that we adopt the song "America the Beautiful" as our national anthem.

6. "Look out for that bump in the road!" shouted Dad.

CD-104311 • © Carson-Dellosa   53

Page 54 — Single Quotation Marks

Name _____

Punctuation

Single Quotation Marks

> When a quoted word or a title is used inside a direct quote, single quotation marks are used.
>> Example: Chelsea said, "I can't seem to spell the word 'peninsula' correctly in this paper."
>
> At the end of a quote, the end punctuation comes between the single and double quotation marks.
>> Example: "Why can't I spell 'peninsula'?" asked Chelsea.

Rewrite each sentence correctly. Add single quotation marks where needed.

1. Filipe said, "I read the article Bike Safety by Mike B. Helmet."
   Filipe said, "I read the article 'Bike Safety' by Mike B. Helmet."

2. "Would you play America the Beautiful on the piano?" asked Sadie.
   "Would you play 'America the Beautiful' on the piano?" asked Sadie.

3. "My essay Life in Antarctica is due tomorrow," explained Ramsey.
   "My essay 'Life in Antarctica' is due tomorrow," explained Ramsey.

4. "How do you spell beluga?" questioned Maja.
   "How do you spell 'beluga'?" questioned Maja.

5. "We have to read the chapter Nighttime again," Merle complained.
   "We have to read the chapter 'Nighttime' again," Merle complained.

6. John told Cindy, "Mom said, You certainly may, when I asked her."
   John told Cindy, "Mom said, 'You certainly may,' when I asked her."

7. Mr. Rich announced, "We will sing the song Spring Day."
   Mr. Rich announced, "We will sing the song 'Spring Day.'"

54   CD-104311 • © Carson-Dellosa

Page 55 — Apostrophes

Name _____

Punctuation

Apostrophes

> Use an apostrophe (') in a contraction to show where a letter or letters have been omitted.
>> Example: Since Andy *wasn't* at home, I *didn't* get to see his new home entertainment center.
>
> Use an apostrophe to show ownership or possession.
>> Example: *Patti's* camera was lying on the backseat of *Mom's* car.
>
> Use an apostrophe to show the plurals of letters, numbers, and words referred to as words. Years can be written with an apostrophe or without.
>> Examples: I received two *B's* in my math classes.
>> The 1990's were exciting years.

Rewrite each sentence, including apostrophes where they are needed.

1. Phil isnt only a singer; hes also a drummer.
   Phil isn't only a singer; he's also a drummer.

2. Omars golf clubs didnt arrive, so he borrowed his friends set.
   Omar's golf clubs didn't arrive, so he borrowed his friend's set.

3. Jamies socks and shoes were found in the gym, so shell need to pick them up from the coachs office.
   Jamie's socks and shoes were found in the gym, so she'll need to pick them up from the coach's office.

4. If I study very hard this semester, Im sure Ill make all As.
   If I study very hard this semester, I'm sure I'll make all A's.

5. I thought that the kite was Noras, but she said that it was her sister-in-laws.
   I thought that the kite was Nora's, but she said that it was her sister-in-law's.

6. Sherrys science classs project grades included 10 As and 10 Bs.
   Sherry's science class's project grades included 10 A's and 10 B's.

CD-104311 • © Carson-Dellosa   55

Name _____ | Punctuation

Semicolons

> The primary purpose of a semicolon (;) is to connect equally important independent clauses that are not joined by *and, but, or, nor, for,* or *yet.*
> Example: Carlos is happy that September is here; he has been looking forward to being in class with his friends.
>
> Use semicolons to separate items that include commas.
> Example: Samantha is planning to invite Sandy, her best friend; Lisette, her next-door neighbor; and Lillie, her cousin.
>
> Use a semicolon between independent clauses that are joined by connecting words such as *however, for example, that is,* and *in fact.* These words are usually followed by commas.
> Example: Kayla's aunt took care of her when she was sick; in fact, she remained at her bedside night and day until she recovered.

Write semicolons and commas in each sentence where needed.

1. Marcy forgot to bring a suitcase; Mindy remembered.

2. So far this month, John has traveled to Jackson, Mississippi; Tallahassee, Florida; and Nashville, Tennessee.

3. Rachel wanted to call her brother on his birthday; however, she was in an airplane most of the day.

4. Casey looked forward to the weekend; his uncle was coming to visit.

5. Jonah's class made lunch for Mr. Burns, the custodian; Mrs. Fry, the head cook; and Miss Bookman, the librarian.

6. Sometimes we stay late after practice; however, we leave when the coach goes home.

56 | CD-104311 • © Carson-Dellosa

Name _____ | Punctuation

Colons

> Use a colon after the main clause to direct the reader's attention to a list.
> Example: Davie's travel kit included these items: shaving cream, a razor, a toothbrush, toothpaste, deodorant, and a comb.
>
> Use a colon to introduce formal quotations.
> Example: The speaker closed with these words: "He was there when I needed him, and he became the guiding force in my life."
>
> Use a colon after the greeting in a business letter.
> Example: Dear Sir:
>
> Use a colon between the hour and minute when writing a time.
> The time is 2:15 P.M.
>
> Do not use a colon immediately after a verb. The colon must be preceded by a full independent clause.
> Example: Raymond's report told about the difficulties of people who were French, Swedish, and German.

Write colons in each phrase or sentence where needed.

1. At 3:00 P.M., everyone in class needs to take the following to the auditorium: a pencil, an eraser, and a notebook.

2. Dear Dr. Wu:

3. These students turned their tests in at the same time: Jeremy, Raul, Stephanie, and Shawna.

4. I need a few things for a new recipe: corn, tomatoes, onions, black beans, and cilantro.

Write a sentence of your own that includes a formal quotation. The first part of the sentence has been started for you. Remember to add a colon where it is needed.

One of my favorite songs begins with these words:

"_____ **Answers will vary.** _____"

CD-104311 • © Carson-Dellosa | 57

Name _____ | Sentences

Parts of a Sentence

> Every sentence has two main parts, a subject and a predicate.
>
> The **simple subject** is the noun or pronoun that tells who or what the sentence is about.
> Example: The older *boys* helped the younger children.
>
> The **complete subject** includes all of the words that identify and modify the simple subject.
> Example: *The older boys* helped the younger children.
>
> The **simple predicate** is the verb or verb phrase that tells something about the subject.
> Example: The older boys *helped* the younger children.
>
> The **complete predicate** includes all of the words that modify the simple predicate.
> Example: The older boys *helped the younger children.*

Circle the complete subject and underline the complete predicate in each sentence.

1. (The robin) is considered a sign of spring in the Midwest.

2. (The Henderson family) just moved into an apartment on the 14th floor.

3. (I) read about the extra traffic that creates problems during the winter.

4. (The U.S. Open) is one of the most prestigious tennis tournaments.

5. (Each member of the Wildcats team) deserves a trophy for his participation and hard work.

6. (Some rivers) flow in a northern direction.

58 | CD-104311 • © Carson-Dellosa

Name _____ | Sentences

Simple Subjects

Circle the simple subject in each sentence.

1. The brightest (star) in the sky was easy to find.

2. Ellen's (business) did well this year.

3. (Someone) needs to volunteer to take tickets for the fund-raiser at the door.

4. Meanwhile, (Adam) thought that he should call his mother.

5. Red, white, and blue (ribbon) decorated the stage for the celebration.

6. The (referee) tossed a coin into the air to determine which team would get the ball first.

7. In the United States, another (name) for the president is commander-in-chief.

8. Fortunately, our (tickets) were for seats close to the playing field.

9. Sadly, (Henry) was out sick today.

10. Can (you) bring your favorite book to school to share with the rest of the class?

CD-104311 • © Carson-Dellosa | 59

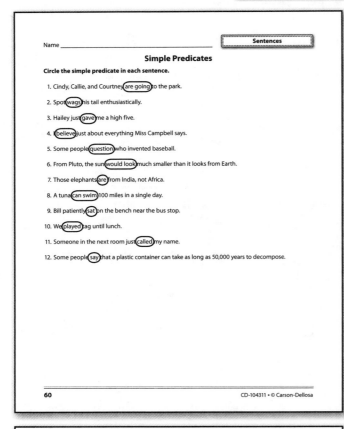

Name _____

Sentences

Simple Predicates

Circle the simple predicate in each sentence.

1. Cindy, Callie, and Courtney (are going) to the park.
2. Spot (wags) his tail enthusiastically.
3. Hailey just (gave) me a high five.
4. I (believe) just about everything Miss Campbell says.
5. Some people (question) who invented baseball.
6. From Pluto, the sun (would look) much smaller than it looks from Earth.
7. Those elephants (are) from India, not Africa.
8. A tuna (can swim) 100 miles in a single day.
9. Bill patiently (sat) on the bench near the bus stop.
10. We (played) tag until lunch.
11. Someone in the next room just (called) my name.
12. Some people (say) that a plastic container can take as long as 50,000 years to decompose.

60   CD-104311 • © Carson-Dellosa

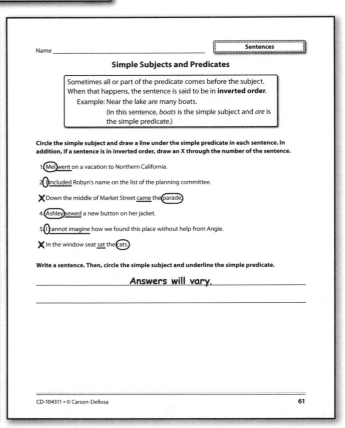

Name _____

Sentences

Simple Subjects and Predicates

> Sometimes all or part of the predicate comes before the subject. When that happens, the sentence is said to be in **inverted order**.
> Example: Near the lake are many boats.
> (In this sentence, *boats* is the simple subject and *are* is the simple predicate.)

Circle the simple subject and draw a line under the simple predicate in each sentence. In addition, if a sentence is in inverted order, draw an X through the number of the sentence.

1. (Mel) went on a vacation to Northern California.
2. (I) included Robyn's name on the list of the planning committee.
X Down the middle of Market Street came the (parade).
4. (Ashley) sewed a new button on her jacket.
5. (I) cannot imagine how we found this place without help from Angie.
X In the window seat sat the (cats).

Write a sentence. Then, circle the simple subject and underline the simple predicate.

_____ Answers will vary. _____

_____

CD-104311 • © Carson-Dellosa   61

Name _____

Sentences

Complete Subjects and Predicates

Write a complete subject or predicate to complete each sentence.

1. _____ Answers will vary. _____ should be enough to fill you up.
2. Our bus ride to Los Angeles, California, _____.
3. The weather for this coming weekend _____.
4. The tallest building downtown _____.
5. _____ brought his dog Bingo to school last Wednesday.
6. _____ placed her award on a shelf.
7. Brittany and her brother Phillip _____.
8. _____ would be a great vacation.

62   CD-104311 • © Carson-Dellosa

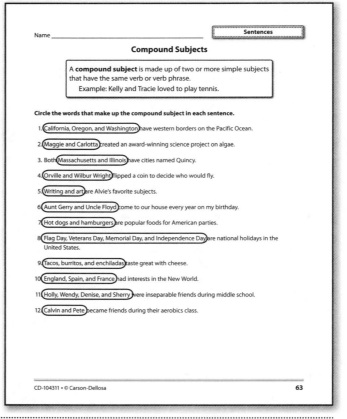

Name _____

Sentences

Compound Subjects

> A **compound subject** is made up of two or more simple subjects that have the same verb or verb phrase.
> Example: Kelly and Tracie loved to play tennis.

Circle the words that make up the compound subject in each sentence.

1. (California, Oregon, and Washington) have western borders on the Pacific Ocean.
2. (Maggie and Carlotta) created an award-winning science project on algae.
3. Both (Massachusetts and Illinois) have cities named Quincy.
4. (Orville and Wilbur Wright) flipped a coin to decide who would fly.
5. (Writing and art) are Alvie's favorite subjects.
6. (Aunt Gerry and Uncle Floyd) come to our house every year on my birthday.
7. (Hot dogs and hamburgers) are popular foods for American parties.
8. (Flag Day, Veterans Day, Memorial Day, and Independence Day) are national holidays in the United States.
9. (Tacos, burritos, and enchiladas) taste great with cheese.
10. (England, Spain, and France) had interests in the New World.
11. (Holly, Wendy, Denise, and Sherry) were inseparable friends during middle school.
12. (Calvin and Pete) became friends during their aerobics class.

CD-104311 • © Carson-Dellosa   63

Name _____ **Sentences**

Compound Predicates

> A **compound predicate** is made up of two or more separate verbs that have the same subject.
> Example: Before going to the game, Matthew finished his homework and ate a healthy dinner.

Circle the words that make up the compound predicate in each sentence.

1. I have saved all of the stories about Marnie's rescue and pasted them into a scrapbook.
2. Charlotte saved her money for two months and then bought a radio for her room.
3. The bluebird population will probably stabilize for a few years and then rise again.
4. Light travels 186,000 miles per second and takes six hours to reach Earth from Pluto.
5. Police fight crime every day and keep our community safe.
6. I can mow the lawn and pick up the grass clippings at the same time with our new lawnmower.
7. Ms. Metcalf gave our class free time today, but she assigned us reading for tomorrow.
8. Karina catches the ball and then brings it back to Halle to play some more.
9. Mom's cookies smelled and tasted great!
10. Kiley ran to the store and returned home in time for her favorite TV show.
11. Jake's dad works as an engineer and coaches our baseball team.
12. Aaron raked the front lawn and then bagged all the leaves.

64   CD-104311 • © Carson-Dellosa

Name _____ **Sentences**

Compound Subjects and Predicates

The sentences below contain either a compound subject or a compound predicate. Circle the words that make up each compound subject and underline the words that make up each compound predicate.

1. Corn and green beans are my two favorite vegetables.
2. The game both entertained and excited the baseball fans.
3. Beth cooked her dinner and then ate it.
4. Diana and I cooked dinner for her parents.
5. Those attending the school picnic sipped lemonade and played games on the soccer field.
6. Vanilla and butter pecan are my two favorite flavors of ice cream.

Write a sentence about your family that has a compound subject.

Answers will vary.

_____

Write a sentence about a close friend that has a compound predicate.

Answers will vary.

_____

CD-104311 • © Carson-Dellosa   65

Name _____ **Sentences**

Subject-Verb Agreement

> The subject and verb of a sentence must agree in number.
>
> Singular subjects must have singular verbs. Most verbs are made singular by adding s or es. *Is, was, has,* and *does* are irregular singular verbs.
> Examples: The road *winds* up the mountain.
> The road *is* bumpy.
>
> Plural subjects must have plural verbs. *Are, were, have,* and *do* are irregular plural verbs.
> Examples: The roads *wind* up the mountain.
> The roads *are* bumpy.

Underline the subject of each sentence. Then, circle the correct form of the verb.

1. Some of the beads (is, are) missing from the necklace.
2. Where (is, are) the gate to her house?
3. Tucson (lies, lie) to the south of Phoenix.
4. A statue of Andrew Jackson (stand, stands) in Jackson Square.
5. The Dodgers, Braves, and Cardinals (is, are) division leaders.

Answers for 6–10 will vary, but some possible verb choices include finish, are, visit, eats, and cheer.

Complete each sentence with a verb that makes sense and agrees in number with the subject.

6. Brittany and Mel _____ their homework immediately after school.
7. If the sheep are in the meadow, the cows _____ in the barn.
8. Tourists _____ warmer climates in the winter.
9. Christie _____ much more slowly than Merilee.
10. The home-team fans always _____ more loudly than the away-team fans.

66   CD-104311 • © Carson-Dellosa

Name _____ **Sentences**

Subject-Verb Agreement

Underline the subject in each sentence. Then, circle the verb that agrees with the subject in number.

1. Gretchen (goes, go) home from college every weekend to see her parents.
2. Carlos and Ben (has been, have been) friends since they were in the third grade.
3. Lindsey (play, plays) on the tennis courts at her apartment building.
4. Both the Yankees and the Mets (calls, call) New York City their home.
5. Trail Ridge Road (winds, wind) its way through Rocky Mountain National Park.
6. The questions on the test (was, were) easy to answer after studying so hard.
7. In the United States, the president and the vice president (runs, run) as a team during a presidential election.
8. Kiley (brings, bring) her pet iguana to school every year for "Pets on Parade Week."

CD-104311 • © Carson-Dellosa   67

Subject-Verb Agreement

Name _____   Sentences

Agreement errors are common when using the contractions *there's*, *here's*, and *where's*.
Examples: Where's the cookies?   (incorrect because *cookies* is plural)
Where's the cookie?   (correct)
Where are the cookies? (correct)

Write a word or pair of words from the box to complete each sentence with the correct subject-verb agreement. You will use some words or pairs more than once.

Where's	Here's	There's
Where are	Here are	There are

1. __Here's/There's__ my mom.   (either is acceptable)
2. __Where are__ your slippers?
3. __Here's/There's__ your lost dog.   (either is acceptable)
4. __Where's__ the dictionary?
5. __Here are/There are__ some books you might like. (either is acceptable)
6. __There are__ drinks on the table.
7. __Where's__ the hospital?
8. __Where are__ my socks?
9. __Here's/There's__ my sister.   (either is acceptable)
10. __Here are/There are__ some tracks.   (either is acceptable)

68   CD-104311 • © Carson-Dellosa

Prepositions

Name _____   Sentences

A **preposition** is a word that shows the relationship between two words in a sentence. It can tell where something is, where something is going, when something happens, or the relationship between a noun or pronoun and another word.
Examples:

about	above	across	after	against
among	at	before	beneath	behind
below	between	beyond	by	down
during	except	for	from	in
inside	into	like	near	of
off	on	out	outside	over
through	to	toward	under	until
up	upon	with	within	without
according to	along with	because of	next to	except for
in addition to	in back of	in front of	in spite of	on account of

When a preposition is used without an object, it becomes an adverb.
Example: Jeff fell *behind* the group of runners. (preposition)
Jeff fell *behind*. (adverb)

Circle the prepositions in each sentence below.

1. Gracie and Helen had not seen each other (for) 50 years.
2. "Tell me (about) Grandpa," said Randy.
3. The water packs were carried (on) their backs.
4. I would go (into) the garden, but it is muddy.
5. Tommy passed the peas (to) his mother.
6. We should meet somewhere (beyond) the city limits.
7. The lights come on automatically (after) sunset.
8. Please put an umbrella (in) the trunk.

CD-104311 • © Carson-Dellosa   69

Prepositional Phrases

Name _____   Sentences

A **prepositional phrase** begins with a preposition and ends with a noun or pronoun. The noun or pronoun in a prepositional phrase is called the object of the preposition. A preposition always has an object. If the word does not have an object, it is not acting as a preposition. A sentence can have more than one prepositional phrase.
Example: The book *on the desk* is mine.
Preposition: on
Object of the preposition: desk
Prepositional phrase: on the desk

Draw a box around each preposition. Circle each object of the preposition. Underline each prepositional phrase. There may be more than one in a sentence.

1. The mare thundered [around] the (corral).
2. Ellen's sunset photograph is hanging [on] our living-room (wall).
3. Kaela's favorite part [of] (dessert) was eating the tip [of] her ice-cream (cone).
4. Jena hugged her horse [with] all her (strength).
5. Gina walked carefully [by] the (edge) [of] the (pond).
6. The washed grapes are [in] the blue (bowl).
7. Maddie fell asleep [with] her (plate) [in] her (lap).
8. Mr. Tennison has a bag [of] jelly beans [in] his desk (drawer).
9. The box [of] (books) is located [behind] the (door).
10. The jar [of] homemade strawberry (jam) did not last long.
11. We are renting the cottage [near] the (dock).
12. Blaine walked [up] the mountain [until] he reached the top.

70   CD-104311 • © Carson-Dellosa

Prepositional Phrases

Name _____   Sentences

Underline each prepositional phrase. Circle each object of the preposition. There may be more than one prepositional phrase in each sentence.

1. We were forced to find shelter from the (weather).
2. In the (afternoon) we drove toward (Memphis).
3. Until that (point) everything had gone well.
4. Rene used the spare key to his parents' (house) that was under the (birdbath).
5. The new dog in our (neighborhood) has tags around its (neck).
6. My desk is covered with paper junk (mail).
7. Dad slept through the whole (show).
8. In (place) of (nails), I used screws.
9. There were boulders and rocks beside the (bridge).
10. Laura was grateful for Rita's (kindness).

CD-104311 • © Carson-Dellosa   71

Name _____   Sentences

Prepositional Phrases

A prepositional phrase can be used to modify a noun, a pronoun, a verb, an adjective, or an adverb.

When a prepositional phrase is used to modify a noun or a pronoun, it is used as an adjective.
  Example: Our run *to the beach* was fun.

When a prepositional phrase is used to modify a verb, an adjective, or an adverb, it is used as an adverb.
  Example: Wendy dove *into the pool.*

Underline the prepositional phrase in each sentence. Write the word *adjective* **or** *adverb* **to tell how the phrase is used.**

1. The papers were organized in alphabetical order. **adverb**
2. She held a glimmer of hope. **adjective**
3. The weeds by the door were brown. **adjective**
4. The tomatoes from our garden were delicious. **adjective**
5. Janie went home with the extra food. **adverb**
6. John hit the ball across the field. **adverb**
7. Sweat was running down her face. **adverb**
8. Please raise the window about halfway. **adverb**
9. Andy found his wallet under his bed. **adverb**
10. The cover of that book is recycled paper. **adjective**

Write a sentence that describes summer. Include at least one prepositional phrase. Underline each prepositional phrase. Write the word *adjective* **or** *adverb* **above each phrase to tell how the phrase is used.**

Answers will vary.

72   CD-104311 • © Carson-Dellosa

Name _____   Sentences

Direct Objects

A **direct object** is the noun or pronoun that receives the action of the verb. It is located in the predicate of a sentence. The predicate is the part of the sentence with a verb.

To locate the direct object, find the verb. Find a noun after the verb that answers *What?* or *Whom?* If the noun is receiving the action of the verb, the noun is the direct object.
  Examples: The ball hit *the target.*
      I gave Chad *some money.*

Underline the verb in each sentence. Circle the direct objects.

1. The courtyard fountain continuously gushed (water).
2. Leona frequently chews (gum).
3. The anxious horse kicked the stall (door).
4. Erica handed Jacob her (paper).
5. Rochelle stowed the (luggage) in the overhead bin.
6. Danielle offered her (carrots) to Jesse.
7. Rosa canceled her (subscription) to the magazine.
8. Yolanda crochets a blue and white (blanket).
9. The hot chicken soup burned April's (tongue).
10. Enrique toasted a (marshmallow) over the campfire.

CD-104311 • © Carson-Dellosa   73

Name _____   Sentences

Direct Objects

Circle the direct object in each sentence.

1. Andy arrived at math class on time, but he forgot a (pencil).
2. Sherrie always helps decorate the family Christmas (tree).
3. Dad grilled the (salmon) on cedar planks.
4. Kelly swept her (room) after she had picked up her clothes.
5. Carrie called (Gretchen) to make plans for Saturday.
6. Jon played his (banjo) for his family.
7. Many people fear the diamondback (rattlesnake).
8. Kerry asked (Aaron) to play a game with him.

Write one sentence with a direct object and one sentence without a direct object.

Answers will vary.

74   CD-104311 • © Carson-Dellosa

Name _____   Sentences

Indirect Objects

An **indirect object** is the noun or pronoun that answers *To whom? For whom? To what?* or *For what?* The indirect object is located in the predicate of the sentence and usually comes between the verb and the direct object.
  Example: Everett handed *Harry* a dollar.

Underline the verbs in each sentence. Circle the indirect objects.

1. José gave his (puppy) a bath.
2. Peter wished his (grandmother) a happy birthday.
3. Walter sold (Alan) the tire swing.
4. The waiter handed (Kent) his dinner platter.
5. Quinn offered (Tommy) her pencil.
6. Aunt May knitted (June) a new yellow scarf.
7. Mr. Slider gave the (chair) a coat of varnish.
8. The students wrote a (family member) a letter.
9. The new neighbor made our (family) stir-fried vegetables.
10. Roberta saved (Rico) some sweet corn.
11. Franco sent his (friends) invitations to his pool party.
12. Allison served her (family) iced lemonade.
13. Lydia handed (Stanton) her beach towel.
14. Alex will save (Jerome) a seat on the bus after school.

CD-104311 • © Carson-Dellosa   75

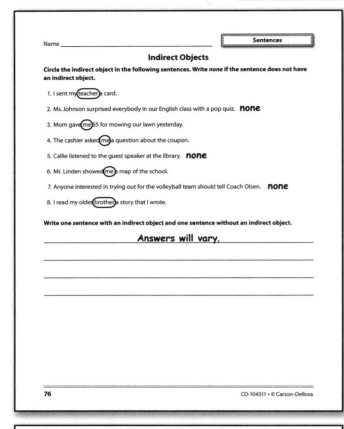

Name _____   Sentences

Indirect Objects

Circle the indirect object in the following sentences. Write *none* **if the sentence does not have an indirect object.**

1. I sent my (teacher) a card.

2. Ms. Johnson surprised everybody in our English class with a pop quiz. **none**

3. Mom gave (me) $5 for mowing our lawn yesterday.

4. The cashier asked (me) a question about the coupon.

5. Callie listened to the guest speaker at the library. **none**

6. Mr. Linden showed (me) a map of the school.

7. Anyone interested in trying out for the volleyball team should tell Coach Olsen. **none**

8. I read my older (brother) a story that I wrote.

Write one sentence with an indirect object and one sentence without an indirect object.

_____ **Answers will vary.** _____

_____

_____

_____

76   CD-104311 • © Carson-Dellosa

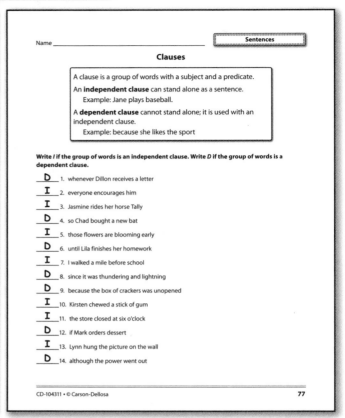

Name _____   Sentences

Clauses

> A clause is a group of words with a subject and a predicate.
> An **independent clause** can stand alone as a sentence.
>   Example: Jane plays baseball.
> A **dependent clause** cannot stand alone; it is used with an independent clause.
>   Example: because she likes the sport

Write *I* **if the group of words is an independent clause. Write** *D* **if the group of words is a dependent clause.**

D 1. whenever Dillon receives a letter

I 2. everyone encourages him

I 3. Jasmine rides her horse Tally

D 4. so Chad bought a new bat

I 5. those flowers are blooming early

D 6. until Lila finishes her homework

I 7. I walked a mile before school

D 8. since it was thundering and lightning

D 9. because the box of crackers was unopened

I 10. Kirsten chewed a stick of gum

I 11. the store closed at six o'clock

D 12. if Mark orders dessert

I 13. Lynn hung the picture on the wall

D 14. although the power went out

CD-104311 • © Carson-Dellosa   77

Name _____   Sentences

Relative Clauses

> A **relative clause** is a dependent clause that modifies a noun or pronoun and begins with a relative pronoun or relative adverb. *Who, whom, whose, that,* and *which* are relative pronouns. *When, where,* and *why* are relative adverbs.
>   Examples: That's the one *that I like best.*
>   Farmers say that spring rains, *which usually begin in April,* are good for the crops.
> Relative clauses are set off with commas if they add information to the sentence that is not necessary.

Underline the relative clause in each sentence.

1. The deck was so wet that it was slippery.

2. The story that Ms. Hobbin read was about monsters.

3. Jenny, who is the fastest girl on the track team, is my best friend.

4. The woman who is wearing white shorts is my mom.

5. We went on a vacation, which was relaxing and fun.

6. Please give this dollar to Holly, who is the treasurer of the student council.

7. The audition will be held at the hotel where many participants are staying.

8. Breakfast begins at 7:00 A.M., when the kitchen opens.

78   CD-104311 • © Carson-Dellosa

Name _____   Sentences

Independent and Dependent Clauses

Write *I* **if the group of words is an independent clause. Write** *D* **if the group of words is a dependent clause.**

I 1. Ryan could only bring two

I 2. last year he tried to visit New York City

I 3. we should not spend time arguing

D 4. because Rachel decided she could come

Circle the independent clause and underline the dependent clause in each sentence.

5. Although I can participate, (I can't stay long.)

6. When Charlie's sister leaves, (Charlie plays with his neighbor.)

7. (She knows more teachers at school) because she is older than her brother.

8. Since the road is new, (it is perfectly smooth.)

Write a sentence that includes both an independent clause and a dependent clause. Circle the independent clause and underline the dependent clause.

_____ **Answers will vary.** _____

_____

_____

CD-104311 • © Carson-Dellosa   79

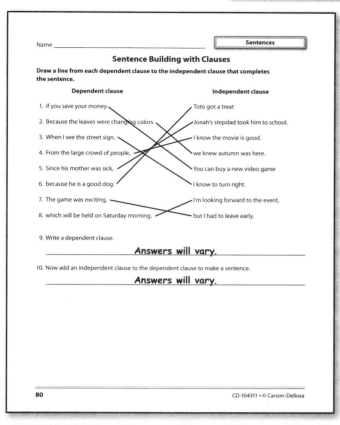

Name _____ [Sentences]

Sentence Building with Clauses

Draw a line from each dependent clause to the independent clause that completes the sentence.

Dependent clause   **Independent clause**

1. if you save your money. — Toto got a treat
2. Because the leaves were changing colors — Jonah's stepdad took him to school.
3. When I see the street sign, — I know the movie is good.
4. From the large crowd of people, — we knew autumn was here.
5. Since his mother was sick, — You can buy a new video game
6. because he is a good dog. — I know to turn right.
7. The game was exciting, — I'm looking forward to the event,
8. which will be held on Saturday morning. — but I had to leave early.

9. Write a dependent clause.

    Answers will vary.

10. Now add an independent clause to the dependent clause to make a sentence.

    Answers will vary.

80   CD-104311 • © Carson-Dellosa

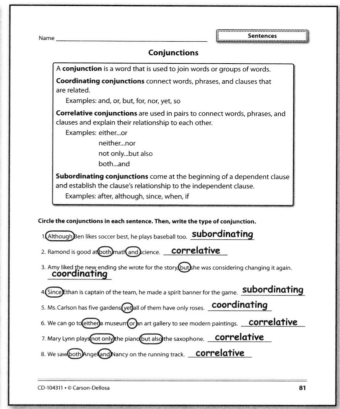

Name _____ [Sentences]

Conjunctions

A **conjunction** is a word that is used to join words or groups of words.
Coordinating conjunctions connect words, phrases, and clauses that are related.
    Examples: and, or, but, for, nor, yet, so
Correlative conjunctions are used in pairs to connect words, phrases, and clauses and explain their relationship to each other.
    Examples: either...or
               neither...nor
               not only...but also
               both...and
Subordinating conjunctions come at the beginning of a dependent clause and establish the clause's relationship to the independent clause.
    Examples: after, although, since, when, if

Circle the conjunctions in each sentence. Then, write the type of conjunction.

1. (Although) Ben likes soccer best, he plays baseball too. **subordinating**
2. Ramond is good at (both) math (and) science. **correlative**
3. Amy liked the new ending she wrote for the story (but) she was considering changing it again. **coordinating**
4. (Since) Ethan is captain of the team, he made a spirit banner for the game. **subordinating**
5. Ms. Carlson has five gardens (yet) all of them have only roses. **coordinating**
6. We can go to (either) a museum (or) an art gallery to see modern paintings. **correlative**
7. Mary Lynn plays (not only) the piano (but also) the saxophone. **correlative**
8. We saw (both) Angel (and) Nancy on the running track. **correlative**

CD-104311 • © Carson-Dellosa   81

Name _____ [Sentences]

Coordinating Conjunctions

Combine each set of sentences using a coordinating conjunction from the box. Write the new sentence on the line. Use each coordinating conjunction once.

| and | or | but | for | yet | so |

1. Devin went swimming in the pool. He did not go swimming in the lake.

    Devin went swimming in the pool, but he did not go swimming in the lake.

2. She enjoys making art. She chooses to spend more time playing sports.

    She enjoys making art, yet she chooses to spend more time playing sports.

3. Josie picked up her backpack. She got on the bus.

    Josie picked up her backpack, and she got on the bus.

4. We can watch the movie. We can meet Joe at the park.

    We can watch a movie, or we can meet Joe at the park.

5. The apples are not mine. I don't know if you can have one.

    The apples are not mine, so I don't know if you can have one.

6. Craig likes riding in airplanes. It makes him feel like he is a bird.

    Craig likes riding in airplanes, for it makes him feel like he is a bird.

82   CD-104311 • © Carson-Dellosa

Name _____ [Sentences]

Correlative Conjunctions

Circle the correlative conjunctions in each sentence.

1. Last night (both) Trey (and) Noreen won awards.
2. (Just as) cars follow street signs, (so) must bikes.
3. (Neither) the map (nor) the itinerary fit in Ophelia's scrapbook.
4. We could use (either) molasses (or) sugar to sweeten the cookies.
5. Bea (not only) decorated the cupcakes (but also) made them from scratch.
6. (Neither) Carlos (nor) Mirabel is going to the meeting tonight.
7. (Either) a period (or) a semicolon can separate a run-on sentence.
8. (Whether) it rains (or) not, we will play soccer.
9. (Both) the paper (and) the project are due on Friday.
10. Mr. Oliver said that I can (either) bring my own pencil (or) borrow one.
11. June wants (both) salt (and) pepper on her vegetables.
12. You need to wear (not only) protective eyeglasses (but also) a helmet.

CD-104311 • © Carson-Dellosa   83

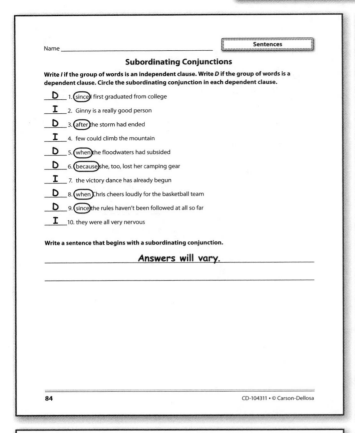

Subordinating Conjunctions

Name _____

Sentences

Write *I* if the group of words is an independent clause. Write *D* if the group of words is a dependent clause. Circle the subordinating conjunction in each dependent clause.

D 1. (since) I first graduated from college

I 2. Ginny is a really good person

D 3. (after) the storm had ended

I 4. few could climb the mountain

D 5. (when) the floodwaters had subsided

D 6. (because) she, too, lost her camping gear

I 7. the victory dance has already begun

D 8. (when) Chris cheers loudly for the basketball team

D 9. (since) the rules haven't been followed at all so far

I 10. they were all very nervous

Write a sentence that begins with a subordinating conjunction.

Answers will vary.

Building Sentences

Name _____

Sentences

Write three sentences. Then, follow the directions for each sentence.

1. Draw a line between the complete subject and the complete predicate.

2. Underline the simple subject.

3. Circle the verb.

4. Write D.O. over the direct object, if there is one.

5. Write I.O. over the indirect object, if there is one.

6. Put a box around each prepositional phrase.

1. _____ **Answers will vary.** _____

2. _____ **Answers will vary.** _____

3. _____ **Answers will vary.** _____

Expanding Sentences

Name _____

Sentences

Sentences can be improved by adding details that will make them more specific and interesting. Details in sentences can answer such questions as *When? Where? What kind? Which one? How often?* and *To what degree?*

Example: The ball left the park. → The towering fly ball was still rising as it went over the fence and left the ballpark.

Expand each of the sentences by adding details that will help answer some of the above questions.

1. The rock broke her window. _____ **Answers will vary.**

2. The woman walked down the street. _____

3. The fire truck responded. _____

4. The basement was flooded. _____

5. My cousin bought a car. _____

6. My stepdad made dinner. _____

7. Susan is nice. _____

Types of Sentences

Name _____

Sentences

A **declarative sentence** makes a statement or states a fact and ends with a period.
　Example: Many have followed the rocky road to success.

An **interrogative sentence** asks a question and ends with a question mark.
　Example: Would you go to the store with me?

An **imperative sentence** gives a command or makes a request and ends with a period.
　Example: Deliver this note to Mrs. Carmen.

An **exclamatory sentence** expresses a strong feeling and ends with an exclamation point.
　Example: What a great day to go to the beach!

Write *D* in front of each declarative sentence, *INT* in front of each interrogative sentence, *IMP* in front of each imperative sentence, and *E* in front of each exclamatory sentence. Then, place the correct punctuation mark at the end of each sentence.

E 1. Living in this city is so exciting **!**

IMP 2. Please repeat what you said earlier **.**

E 3. What an amazing performance James gave **!**

D 4. Jeff started playing golf at a young age **.**

INT 5. Will you pass the peas, please **?**

IMP 6. Lay your pencil down when you are finished **.**

INT 7. Did you get to see Will's performance **?**

E 8. I love my baby sister so much **!**

D 9. Logan sent an invitation to Anna through e-mail **.**

E 10. What a beautiful ship it was **!**

INT 11. Will you give me a helping hand **?**

E 12. I am so glad you are coming to my concert **!**

Name _____ Sentences

Types of Sentences

Write the correct punctuation mark at the end of each sentence.

1. Which of these sentences is correct **?**

2. Sarah's motivation was clear **.**

3. The price of rice is consistent **.**

4. Shake it off **!**

5. If I go, will you come with me **?**

6. Rutherford B. Hayes won one of the most hotly contested presidential races in U.S. history **.**

7. Your shirt is a nice color **.**

8. As they say in show business, "Break a leg **!** "

9. The waves on the lake are high today **.**

10. I can't believe my ears **!**

88   CD-104311 • © Carson-Dellosa

Name _____ Sentences

Run-On Sentences

A **run-on sentence** occurs when two or more sentences are run together without proper punctuation.
    Example: I like the way you draw, I like the colors you use in your paintings.

A run-on sentence can be corrected by separating it into two sentences or by separating the two clauses with a semicolon or a comma and a conjunction.
    Example: I like the way you draw. I like the colors you use in your paintings.
    Example: I like the way you draw, and I like the colors you use in your paintings.
    Example: I like the way you draw; I like the colors you use in your paintings.

Correct each run-on sentence.

1. My house is near a market I can walk to get a sandwich.
    Answers will vary.

2. The man who makes the sandwiches is named Dan he is really nice he gives me extra pickles.
    Answers will vary.

3. Sometimes I ride my bike instead of walking I can get there faster I can carry groceries in my basket.
    Answers will vary.

4. On the way home from the market, I start nibbling on fresh vegetables that are grown by local farmers who brought them to the market to sell and if you get there early enough you can see them unloading their trucks.
    Answers will vary.

CD-104311 • © Carson-Dellosa   89

Name _____ Sentences

Sentence Fragments

Remember, a complete sentence requires both a subject and a predicate. A **sentence fragment** is an incomplete sentence, or a sentence without a subject or a predicate.
    Examples: Played a great match but lost. (no subject)
    Samantha, my sister. (no predicate)

Write C on the line if the group of words is a complete sentence. Write F on the line if the group of words is a sentence fragment.

C 1. I plan to be there before anyone else.

C 2. If you go camping, be certain you take a warm sleeping bag.

F 3. Behind the barn.

F 4. When the game ended.

C 5. The jockey mounted his horse.

F 6. Whether there is enough food or not.

F 7. Swimming in the lake.

C 8. The concert ended too soon.

Rewrite each of these sentence fragments as complete sentences.

9. From high atop the stadium.
    Answers will vary.

10. Hidden under the basket.
    Answers will vary.

90   CD-104311 • © Carson-Dellosa

Name _____ Sentences

Active and Passive Voice

In the **active voice**, the subject is doing the action.
    Example: Todd fixed Mrs. Horvath's window.

In the **passive voice**, the subject is being acted upon.
    Example: Mrs. Horvath's window was fixed by Todd.

Rewrite each sentence that is in the active voice into the passive voice. Rewrite each sentence that is in the passive voice into the active voice.

1. Experiments have been conducted by students to test the hypothesis.
    Students have conducted experiments to test the hypothesis.

2. Over two-thirds of the applicants passed the exam.
    The exam was passed by over two-thirds of the applicants.

3. The results of the research will be published in the next issue of the journal.
    The researchers will publish their results in the next issue of the journal.

4. The school secretary notified the teacher that one student was absent.
    The teacher was notified by the school secretary that one student was absent.

5. The vegetarian pizza was enjoyed by all of my friends.
    All of my friends enjoyed the vegetarian pizza.

6. Tim hammered the nail into the timber.
    The nail was hammered into the timber by Tim.

CD-104311 • © Carson-Dellosa   91

Name _____

Word Study

Double Negatives

Negatives are words that usually begin with the letter *n*; *no, none, not, nobody, nothing, never, neither,* and *no one* are examples of negatives.

Proper grammar usage of a negative word avoids the use of two in the same sentence.

Example: I do not want nothing in this bag except groceries!   (incorrect)
I do not want anything in this bag except groceries!   (correct)

However, if a comma follows a negative, it is acceptable to use another negative in the same sentence.

Example: No, Shannon does not want to go to the park today.

Some negatives that do not begin with the letter *n* include *scarcely, hardly,* and *barely.*

Rewrite each sentence to correct the double negatives.

1. Sidney couldn't do nothing with her hair.
_____ **Answers will vary.** _____

2. Todd didn't have no second thoughts about the decision he made.
_____

3. No, Celia didn't see nobody else at the market.
_____

4. Kevin could not barely see the road because of the heavy snow.
_____

5. Mia hasn't received no mail in more than a week.
_____

6. Parker wasn't planning no visit to California in the near future.
_____

92   CD-104311 • © Carson-Dellosa

Name _____

Word Study

Doesn't and *Don't*

Doesn't is the contraction of *does not*. It should be used with singular nouns and the pronouns *he, she,* and *it.*
Example: Madeline doesn't want to go.

Don't is the contraction of *do not*. It should be used with plural nouns and the pronouns *I, you, we,* and *they.*
Example: The students in Ms. Li's class don't all get out at 3:00 P.M.

Circle the correct contraction in each sentence.

1. Why (doesn't) don't) Cassie ever arrive on time?

2. It (doesn't) don't) happen very often.

3. Terry and I (doesn't (don't) think it will rain today.

4. This math problem (doesn't) don't) fit with the others.

5. This battery (doesn't) don't) work.

6. Becca and Royce (doesn't, (don't) want to eat too late.

7. Why (doesn't (don't) you and your friend carpool?

8. Gordon (doesn't) don't) like the idea of putting ketchup on eggs.

9. Golfers (doesn't (don't) play when it is stormy.

10. My rabbit (doesn't) don't) like to eat celery.

11. This nail (doesn't) don't) work for hanging that picture.

12. Romero and Holly (doesn't (don't) care much for dessert.

CD-104311 • © Carson-Dellosa   93

Name _____

Word Study

Who and *Whom*

Use *who* as a subject pronoun. *Whoever* can also be used as a subject.
Examples: *Who* came to the graduation party?
Whoever needs extra help can see me after class.

Use *whom* as an object pronoun. *Whomever* can also be used as an object pronoun.
Examples: *Whom* did you bring home for dinner?
The trophy is for *whomever* the judges select.

Use *whom* as the object of a preposition.
Example: To *whom* do you wish me to give this message?

Write either *who* or *whom* to complete each sentence.

1. **Who** made the first moon landing?

2. **Whom** do you like the best among the candidates?

3. **Who** is your very best friend in the whole world?

4. **Who** won the gold medal?

5. **Who** does Ryan think will be the best choice for the math contest?

6. **Who** was the man she saw walking his dog?

7. **Whom** shall I call in case of an emergency?

8. He is the person **who** is always late!

9. One of the boys **whom** we know is very tall.

10. A teacher **whom** we admire spoke at our graduation.

Write a sentence of your own in which you use either *who* or *whom* correctly.
_____ **Answers will vary.** _____

94   CD-104311 • © Carson-Dellosa

Name _____

Word Study

Lie/Lay and *May/Can*

Lie means "to recline" and does not take a direct object.
Example: Why won't you *lie* down and rest?

Lay means "to place" and does take a direct object.
Example: When will they *lay* your new carpet?

Use *may* to ask permission.
Example: *May* I have a piece of that pizza?

Use *can* to express the ability to do something.
Example: Phil *can* play golf very well.

Circle the correct choice for each of the following.

1. Bingo, (lie) lay) down!

2. Toto (may (can) do several tricks if you give him a reward for his actions.

3. Mom, (may) can) Amy spend the night on Friday?

4. No one (may (can) understand the problem like Evelyn!

5. Janie (may (can) return to work when she is feeling well again.

6. If you see Mandy, you (may) can) offer her a ride home.

7. Please (lie (lay) the paper on the stairs.

8. You may (lie (lay) the magazine on the table when you're finished looking at it.

9. I (may (can) only reach the green if I hit the ball a long way!

10. The cat wants to (lie) lay) down on the blanket.

Write a sentence that includes the word *lie*.
_____ **Answers will vary.** _____

Write a sentence that includes the word *lay*.
_____ **Answers will vary.** _____

CD-104311 • © Carson-Dellosa   95

That and Which

Name _____ **Word Study**

> The pronouns *that* and *which* can help you decide if you need commas.
>
> Use *that* and no comma when the modifier is necessary for meaning. Such clauses that are necessary to define the meaning are called restrictive clauses and do not require commas.
>
>   Example: Circle the answer that best answers each question.
>
> Use *which* and a comma or commas when the modifier is not necessary for meaning. Such clauses are called nonrestrictive clauses and require commas.
>
>   Example: The temperature, which is normal for this time of year, is in the high 80s.

Circle the correct word, *that* or *which*, for each sentence.

1. Sarah rode the bicycle (**that**, which) belonged to her brother.

2. Bicycles, (that, **which**) are relatively inexpensive, provide transportation and exercise.

3. The band (**that**, which) will perform first tonight is from Kansas City, Missouri.

4. The flute (**that**, which) Jerry accidentally dropped cannot be fixed by this evening.

5. Babe Ruth's home-run record, (that, **which**) now has been broken several times, stood for over three decades.

6. I am looking for a magazine (**that**, which) reviews new songs.

Write a sentence using *that*.

         Answers will vary.

Write a sentence using *which*.

         Answers will vary.

96   CD-104311 • © Carson-Dellosa

Synonyms and Antonyms

Name _____ **Word Study**

> A **synonym** is a word that has the same or nearly the same meaning as another word.
>   Examples: earth = soil
>   away = absent
>
> An **antonym** is a word that has the opposite meaning of another word.
>   Examples: tall ≠ short
>   happy ≠ sad

Answers will vary, but these are examples.

Write a synonym for the underlined word in each sentence.

1. When you launder your clothes, be certain to use soap. **wash**

2. Winning the lottery was exciting for Matthew. **exhilarating**

3. The winter day was dreary. **nasty**

Write a synonym for each of the following words.

4. gather	**collect**	7. quickly	**rapidly**
5. jump	**leap**	8. tired	**weary**
6. crawl	**inch**	9. sprint	**run**

Write an antonym for the underlined word in each sentence.

10. The morning rush-hour traffic created a real mess! **evening**

11. With camera in hand, the photographer was there to capture the beautiful sunset. **sunrise**

12. I can't imagine a more difficult dilemma. **pleasant**

Write an antonym for each of the following words.

13. straight	**crooked**	16. horrible	**wonderful**
14. narrow	**wide**	17. open	**close**
15. near	**distant**	18. find	**lose**

CD-104311 • © Carson-Dellosa   97

Homophones and Homographs

Name _____ **Word Study**

> A **homophone** is a word that sounds the same as another word but has a different spelling and a different meaning.
>   Examples: pail, pale
>   know, no
>
> A **homograph** is a word that has the exact same spelling as another word but has a different meaning and sometimes has a different pronunciation.
>   Example: bank: a place where people keep their money
>   bank: the land along the sides of a river

Circle the correct homophone or homophones to complete each sentence.

1. Tanya (new, **knew**) how to get along with (**new**, knew) people she met.

2. The (our, **hour**) hand on (**our**, hour) new clock doesn't move correctly.

3. I like to (**read**, reed) magazines about sports.

4. You can (**buy**, by) a good used TV in the store next (**to**, two, too) the shopping mall.

5. Spencer and Jack invited me to come to (there, **their**) house after school.

6. Mrs. Brinks told her students to bring (to, **two**, too) pencils to class for the test.

7. I (**see**, sea) a beautiful sunset down by the (see, **sea**) every night.

8. Our cat, Cosby, sometimes chases his (tale, **tail**).

Use one of the homographs from the box to complete each sentence.

vault	checks	safe	interest

9. Raul was **safe** at second base.

10. Mr. Beamon **checks** our assignments every day for errors.

11. Rae Ann uses a long pole to **vault** over the bar.

12. The critic looked at the new painting with great **interest**.

98   CD-104311 • © Carson-Dellosa

Synonyms, Antonyms, Homonyms, and Homographs

Name _____ **Word Study**

If the underlined words in each sentence are synonyms, write *S*. If they are antonyms, write *A*. If they are homophones, write *HP*. If they are homographs, write *HG*.

HP 1. The wind blew the puffy clouds across the blue sky.

HG 2. I can't lie; it's impossible for my dog to lie still.

A 3. It was unknown who won the famous tournament.

S 4. Tonya will pursue a degree in biology, but first she must seek a college loan.

S 5. To squeeze the orange well, you have to compress the clamp all the way.

HP 6. As J. J. read the book, he noticed a red spot on the page.

HG 7. Everything will be fine, even if I have to pay a fine.

A 8. The flowers are so beautiful, but the weeds are ugly!

S 9. The rigid piece of wood made the position of the table's leg unalterable.

A 10. I thought I could detect a slight smile behind the frown on Mindy's face.

CD-104311 • © Carson-Dellosa   99

Name _____ Word Study

Idioms

An **idiom** is an expression that has a meaning different from the usual meanings of the words within the expression.
Example: to fly off the handle = to lose control of one's temper

Underline each idiom. Then, write what you think it means.

1. The city council was on the fence about building the new city hall.

Answers will vary.

2. Mr. Banks was commenting on the nice weather, when it began to rain out of the blue.

_____

3. Maya was out of sight, out of mind; Randy soon forgot all about her.

_____

4. Sam was on pins and needles waiting for the results from the election.

_____

5. Liz knew that a penny saved is a penny earned, so she always cooked lunch at home instead of eating out.

_____

6. Andy went the extra mile; he learned the entire poem instead of just one stanza.

_____

Write a sentence using an idiom you have heard.

Answers will vary.

_____

_____

Name _____ Writing

Business Letters

Business letters have seven parts: return address, date, inside address, greeting, body, closing, and signature.

The **return address** is the writer's address. It includes the writer's name, street address, city, state, and zip code.

The **date** appears directly below the return address.

The **inside address** includes the name of the person to whom the letter is being written, his or her company name, and the street address, city, state, and zip code.

The **greeting** is a formal beginning to the letter and includes the person's title and last name followed by a colon.

The **body** is the main content of the letter.

The **closing** is a formal end to the letter. *Sincerely* is an appropriate closing.

The **signature** is the writer's full name and comes at the end of the letter.

Label the parts of the business letter.

Miss Patricia Boyd
243 Oak Avenue
Thisplace, Ohio 12345   **return address**

Monday, October 3, 2010   **date**

Mrs. G. H. Wells
Chamber of Commerce
33 Icy Avenue
Colder, Alaska 11111   **inside address**

Dear Mrs G. H. Wells: **greeting**

Hello. I am writing this letter to request information about your city. Mr. Smarts, my social studies teacher, said that many chambers of commerce can send information about their towns. I would like any materials you can send, please.   **body**

Sincerely,   **closing**

Patricia Boyd   **signature**

Name _____ Writing

Business Letters

Write a business letter.

_____
_____
_____

Answers will vary but should have all components of a business letter.

_____

_____

_____

_____

_____

_____

_____

_____

_____

_____

_____
_____

Name _____ Writing

Writing Dialogue

When writing a conversation, begin a new paragraph every time the speaker changes.
Example:
"Mark, did you go to the basketball game yesterday?" asked Eddie.
"Yes, I did," answered Mark.
"Did you see Max make that layup? It was great!"
"You bet," said Mark. "It was one in a million."

Rewrite the following conversation using the appropriate punctuation.

Boy, am I in trouble cried Joan. What's the problem asked Virginia. I left my house key in my room and now I can't get in. Mom won't be home for two more hours, Joan said. Virginia said Let's leave a note on your door, then go to my house. Your mom can pick you up there. Great idea said Joan.

"Boy, am I in trouble!" cried Joan.

"What's the problem?" asked Virginia.

"I left my house key in my room, and now I can't get in. Mom won't be home for two more hours," Joan said.

Virginia said, "Let's leave a note on your door, then go to my house. Your mom can pick you up there."

"Great idea!" said Joan.

Mr. Jones	Lincoln Memorial	we	they
Don	Central Cafe	me	it
Ms. Ming	Texas	you	he
Amanda	Los Angeles	I	she

us	their	was	might
them	my	are	have
her	her	am	has
him	his	is	were

© CD

seem

where

ocean

to go

© CD

© CD

© CD

© CD

will

an

newspaper

to disappear

© CD

© CD

© CD

© CD

been

the

air

to request

© CD

© CD

© CD

© CD

could

a

when

to refuse

© CD

© CD

© CD

© CD

nobody	smallest	badly	now
obvious	smaller	bad	at
chosen	biggest	good	never
gone	bigger	well	sometimes

© CD